I DESERTED HITLER

Memoirs of Bruno J. Trappmann

by Nancy F. Inglis

Lore, Mother, Hilde and me.

This book is dedicated to all those brave souls who opposed and fought Hitler and his despicable henchmen, and who helped others to escape his predatory clutches.

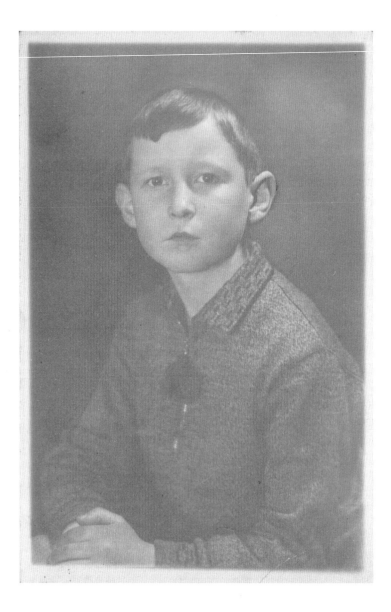

CONTENTS

PREFACE

I look back on my life with Bruno Trappmann, and recognise in him the substance of an extraordinary man. I met him one night at the Jazz Club in Melbourne. I felt at once his spontaneity, no posturing—his whole persona was 'This is who and what I am'. He grew up in Nazi Germany but there was little, if any, rigid German personality about him. His integrity was obvious, he was purely genuine, incapable of faking emotion. His laughter would burst out of him or his indignation would reach explosion point over top-level stupidity or injustices.

His strong conviction that it was immoral to kill another human being steeled his nerves to opt out of the front line in Stalingrad, after being drafted into the German army, unwilling to risk his life to further Hitler's evil plan to conquer the Soviet Union (the 'bread basket of Europe'). How he survived as a deserter in Nazi Germany, with its active and predatory Gestapo, is something I marvel at.

Preface

He lived life to no strict pattern. Work he tackled with great zest, relaxing with joyful jazz in his ears (no Wagner for Bruno!) and a beer at his elbow. At his heart's core was a simple belief in the truth of things. He was not one for any kind of subterfuge, quickly picking the genuine man from the charlatan, the altruistic doctor from the quack. When Bruno told me he loved me with all his heart, joy enveloped me like a warm blanket. We spent 25 years together in good partnership.

He held onto a passionate belief in the rights of humans to individual freedom, not to be controlled or inhibited by authorities. He suffered, first under Nazism, then less rigidly but nonetheless strictly under the Soviet post-war occupation of Eastern Germany. Because he experienced a different society in Australia where more freedom was offered the individual, he judged it the best country in the world.

He met life's misadventures with resourcefulness and courage. I loved and admired him for it and when misfortune struck, confining him to a wheelchair with both legs amputated, his implacable will demanded that he still be 'in the middle of life'. I cannot dismiss such a man from the honour roll of brave men.

To share life with me on our farm in the middle of nature was his fulfillment, his ultimate utopia, his 'paradise'. Bruno saw, in its fascinating design, the hand of a Higher Being. His ashes are strewn where he wished them to be, among the ferns, the trees and the native grasses on the rise opposite our home from where, for years, he gazed out in appreciation and contentment.

Nancy F. Inglis

CHILDHOOD

When I was four years old, my mother pulled a hat on my head, to protect my fair skin and hair, before I played in the garden and said to me, 'I pray they won't ever take you for a soldier!' But Mother's prayer was never answered.

We didn't know it then, but Adolph Hitler would soon want every fit German youth for his armies. When I was old enough, I was drafted, together with all my schoolmates, firstly into the Reichsarbeitdienst or RAD (German National Work Service), then into the regular German army. Soon, I was on the Russian Front going as far into that vast country as Stalingrad. But my story starts before this, in Germany during the 1920s and 30s.

I was born on the river Rhine in 1920. When I turned two, we moved to Nienburg, a town in middle Germany, where my mother had grown up. I don't remember the move much except for one incident when I found myself outside a big door with shop windows on both sides. I didn't know where I was, so I cried and suddenly two ladies opened the door. 'Oh, poor little boy, we'll find your mother,' one said and the other, staring hard at me, suddenly exclaimed, 'Helen, it's little Bruno!' So I was swept up and taken inside our new house, big, dark and strange, by my two aunts, Anne and Helen.

The home where I grew up.

The house we now lived in, in Nienburg, was bought by my mother's father, my grandfather, in the mid-1800s. The triple-storey house stood on wide acres of good farm land. When Grandfather became too old to farm, he offered half of the land to the local blacksmith and separated the two sections with a high brick wall. I remember, as a boy, climbing to the top of this wall, gazing about me in delight, feeling as though I owned the sky and the trees and all the birds. Years later, my ease with heights helped me escape from a prison camp after long weeks of captivity, but I will elaborate on that later.

When Grandfather converted a front section of the big house into a textile shop, my aunts, Helen and Anne, managed it for him until they were too old, then Mother took over.

My attractive young mother.

I had one of the best mothers in the world. After her day's work in the shop, Mother would put me on her back and laugh and play with me. During the day, I spent a lot of time alone, while Mother worked. I learnt to amuse myself, trundling my little three-wheeler bike around the large square back garden of our solid brick mansion. Dr Haensch, a medical practitioner, and Dr Heutling, a dentist, had flats on the ground floor and other tenants lived on the second floor. Store sheds full of fruit lined the sides of the garden, ready for winter consumption and I can remember the lovely smell of the apples and pears. Alongside that was the dark coal shed, stacked full of briquettes for the tenants.

I was fascinated most by the lumber room, where my friend Paul and I had fun pulling all sorts of items out of boxes stored in the room. We'd play dress-ups with crinolines and old suits, hats and wigs, which we had found crammed in the boxes. Another great interest was a fish pond in the garden, where I spent a lot of time catching newts and other aquatic life, putting them in bottles to study their strange shapes.

Mother was happy for me to amuse myself, as she had much on her mind. My father Wilhelm Trappmann suffered from a terminal illness. He spent long hours in the large, dark front bedroom in a bed of his own. His pale face never lost its serious expression; I can't recall ever seeing him smile. He seldom spoke to me and never took any real interest in what I did. When he arose and dressed in one of his dark, well-tailored suits, he looked very distinguished—a good-looking, middle-class man. But his illness made the gap of ten years between him and my mother seem much more.

Father was a violin virtuoso and his musical talent was recognised by Herr Alfred Krupp, known as the 'armaments king' because of the Krupp family's success manufacturing ammunition and armaments, and he paid for his musical education. Subsequently Father gave regular violin recitals for Herr Krupp and his guests, at the Krupp's palatial mansion.

One day, Father picked up my hand in his long, thin, cold one and dropped it in disgust saying, 'You will never play a violin with those stubby fingers.' He gave me a little violin but never instructed me how to play. Always he was preoccupied with his personal problems, so when I arrived late in his life there was nothing left over for me.

I was six years old when my father died. Mother was a young widow of 46, but she never remarried and I grew up entirely surrounded by females, who alternately bossed and smothered me: Aunt Anne, Aunt Helen, my two sisters, Hildegard and Lore (both more than 10 years my senior) and lastly Bertha, our maidservant. I was bombarded with unwelcome kisses. Everywhere I looked there was a woman telling me what to do. It was 'Don't touch!' and 'Go outside and play' or 'Come here and have your dinner'. Often I climbed up the big pear tree to keep out of the way of them all.

I much preferred to be outside in the freedom of the outdoors. Our home was sombre and dark, with paintings by famous artists from the Düsseldorf school hung all over the walls. I didn't like the masterpieces; they looked old and dreary, no brightness and life in them. Nor did I like the classical music my two old aunts listened to as they knitted. Sometimes Aunt Anne would say, 'I'm thirsty, go to the hotel Bruno and bring me a glass of beer.' It was close by, so off I'd go and bring back a foaming drink, running with it so the head would not go flat. All my life I've been a beer drinker and even at that early age, I liked the malt smell of beer.

My sister Hildegard, or Hilde, brought some life into our home. My remarkable sister was 12 years my senior, aflame with youth and energy, going forward at top speed towards the latest thing. She was tall and graceful, her dark hair lustrous and springy, her grey-green eyes sparkling with mischievous life. I became accustomed to the line of aspiring boyfriends following her around. Hilly went to a private higher education school in Bernberg where she learned languages and chose a commercial course to train her for office work. Having her around helped to dispel the sombre flatness pervading the home. She later found work for a doctor in Erfurt, 300 kilometres (186 miles) away and when I was tucked up in bed at night, I could hear her coming in late from the train, whistling as she walked home. I loved her, she was so lively, dancing and listening to the English jazz programs over the radio. My other sister, Lore, worked in the shop with mother; I loved her too but she was quieter, more serious.

Hilde and Lore, stealing my thunder.

When I turned seven, I began primary school and Mother treated this as a most important day in my life. Traditionally, children on their first school day in Germany took a large cone, called a *schultüte* (a school cone), filled with sweets, to share around. Mother was generous; she made a cone as tall as myself and filled it with sweets. I was dressed neatly in new school clothes and Mother arranged for a photographer to come and take a photo of me.

Lore with little 'bübchen'.

Unbeknownst to her, Hilde schemed to feature in the photo. She was an attractive girl of 19 and people called her 'the swan' because of her slender, graceful neck. Having donned her best dress, silk stockings and a pair of smart shoes with straps over her insteps, she was ready. In this fetching regalia, with a slim hand placed provocatively on a shapely hip and a leg turned to exhibit a slender ankle, she instructed the photographer to snap the picture. I stood between my two sisters, feeling dwarfed by their adorned and scented bodies.

Mother was furious when she saw the photograph.

'What were you doing there,' I heard Mother scolding my sisters. 'It was not for you to be seen, it was Bruno's first day at school and you were putting yourselves into it, acting like screen sirens!'

Because Mother managed the shop and had no time to pick me up from school, Lore came once a month, meeting me at the gate, kissing me and calling me *bübchen* (sweet little baby), oblivious of my acute embarrassment. The other kids translated it as *pübshen* (little fart) and had great fun teasing me. I hated my big sister coming, but I couldn't say anything to hurt her feelings.

My friend Paul didn't tease me. He lived next door to me, in a working-class home, a down-to-earth lively place, so different from mine. I longed to join Paul and the other street kids and play with them in the street, without worrying about keeping my good clothes clean.

One of the jobs the neighbourhood children did was to collect manure. During my childhood in Nienburg, there were no motor cars, just farmers' carts pulled by a couple of draught horses that heaped mounds of manure in the streets every day. The kids had the job of collecting manure in their handcarts and bringing it back for their fathers' gardens.

I was glad one day when Paul called me to help him collect horse 'apples'. I ran alongside him, happy to be accepted into the street life.

A horse and cart passed and left a big, juicy, steaming pile of dung in the middle of the road, some of the 'apples' bigger than a man's fist. I raced over and grabbed the biggest and held it up.

'Look what I've got!', I yelled excitedly. Other kids looked at me in amazement and fell about laughing.

Childhood

'Pfui, pfui! He's got shit on his hands! We'll tell his mother!'

I seized Paul's cart and pulled it willingly, so happy I had grabbed the biggest horse apple of the lot. Mother shared none of my triumph, confronting me with a grim face.

'Look at you! I know all about it. Go to the bathroom, Bertha will scrub you clean!' Suddenly I felt very ashamed, Bertha was choking back gusts of laughter as she bathed me and threw out my smelly clothes.

My free spirit quite often landed me in trouble, something I shared with Paul. His fingers poked into everything and one day he offered me a sample of his father's chewing tobacco.

'Taste it,' he said, his eyes dancing. I took a pinch of the greasy substance, it smelt like Paul's father and I spat it out. Postmaster Gotsch, Paul's father, delivered the daily letter post for Nienburg and he was a familiar figure, tramping round the streets. In winter, the black bristly growth on his upper lip grew white with snowflakes. I glimpsed him shaving once, using a sharp open blade and a moustache shield to save the precious bristles from an accidental trim. Herr Gotsch was a big, loud-voiced man, so different from my father—I never felt at ease with him.

After I tried the tobacco, Paul said, laughing, 'Now I'll give you something nice.' He climbed onto a chair and reached for a bottle of his father's blackcurrant wine on the top pantry shelf. It tasted nice and strong and we laughed and staggered about pretending to be drunk. When no one was around, we would take it down from the shelf and have sly sips of it and soon the level in the bottle went down. Paul became worried, his father was throwing a party for his older brother Franz's birthday, and the now-half empty bottle would be discovered.

'Fill it up with water,' I replied confidently. On the night of the party, Postmaster Gotsch produced his bottle with a flourish, Paul and I stood

19

nervously in a corner, hoping the watered product would pass unnoticed. His father filled his guests' glasses, boasting of the wine's rare quality.

Suddenly, I thought it a good idea to go, and we sneaked outside just in time to hear Postmaster Gotsch roaring and cursing from the party room. Paul whimpered, imagining his father's strap on his back. but he escaped a thrashing, his innocent brother Franz receiving the fire of his father's wrath. Unrepentant, Paul and I felt very clever, but it was harder to get away with mischief at school.

I didn't like school much. It commenced at 7 a.m. and the hours dragged by till it finished at 1 p.m. Reluctant to get up and face the school morning, I lay in bed and listened to the bustle of life going on in the streets outside our house. I heard Herr Weider opening his butcher shop next to us and his mother's voice calling her geese, 'Ale ale kum!' (Old one, old one, come!). She brought her flock down to the river Bode, the old goose leading all her little goslings, waddling across the road in perfect safety. In our town, geese and ducks going to and from the river or waterholes had right-of-way. All day Frau Weider's geese were at the river, swimming and eating and diving, then at dusk they shook their feathers and returned home, waddling behind the old one. I wished I could go to the river and play, but already Mother was calling me to get up and dress for school.

The first teacher I had was Kurt Neubauer, a tenant in our house. I didn't like him; he was quick-tempered and very ready with his cane, although he rarely touched me. Bad policy I guess, living as he did in Mother's house. Only once he thrashed me and badly. I didn't have to tell Mother, the red marks were still across my back when I had my evening bath. She was appalled but didn't complain to Herr Neubauer, not like Paul's mother. She marched up and confronted the schoolmaster, shaking a well-worn slipper in the hot-headed teacher's face, threatening him with her husband's fists. Herr Neubauer laid off the cane for a while but nothing really changed.

One school subject I did like was the study of nature. I would take charge of the class when we walked in the forests. I loved sniffing the tangy air and finding the names of all the species growing there. The forest seemed to talk to me, I loved every forest tree and often I left home and walked to it over the Saale bridge. I collected mushrooms in season and taught myself the names of the many wild grasses. In summer, Paul and I swam in the clear river pools.

As I walked further into the forest, deer would cross my path and fill my heart with pleasure. It was a beautiful sight to see them running together, skimming over the ground on long, slender legs. Sometimes I saw a hare sitting with his ears pointed straight up, then running in fright, zigzagging to trick anyone who might have a bullet for him. Often I did not want to go home. I imagined living in the middle of the forest, like Hansel and Gretel.

Herr Erich Masser, our teacher for nature study did not have long to give to his profession, as a few years later he was in the Lutwaffe and was shot down by enemy aircraft in the 'Battle for Britain'. One day he asked the class pupils what career they wished to follow. I said, 'I want to be a *naturforscher* (a nature investigator).' The whole class rocked with laughter, even the teacher smirked and after that the kids called me 'nature farter'.

Every week, a Lutheran priest, Pastor Koch, came to the school to give us a boring lesson on theology, even though he put a great deal of righteous fire into his subject. To make it more interesting, we used to bet each other how many times he would thump the master's desk, using it as his pulpit. I remember, one day after a particularly fiery oration that left him physically weak, he took off his high starched hat and went for a drink at the fountain. Franz, a little imp of a kid, skipped out of his desk to where Pastor Koch had carefully laid his hat and squashed it flat. It was so funny, I couldn't stop laughing; it seemed an outrageous blow to strike at Pastor Koch's dignified status. When he came back and saw his holy headpiece flattened like a pancake, his glittering eyes roved over the class looking for the guilty boy. He heard and saw my spluttering merriment and bore down on me, forgetful of his 'peaceful man of God' role and gave me a couple of hearty whacks over my ears.

On another occasion, Pastor Koch solemnly intoned 'Man doth not live by bread alone'. He glanced around and picked on Fritz, a boy whose father was the town butcher, with a reputation for making an interesting range of small goods. 'Now boy, what does man require to live a good and pious life?' Up jumps Fritz, confident he had the right answer.

'Sausages' he burst out happily.

These light spots helped me get through my lessons, but most days I couldn't leave school fast enough. Sometimes I felt I was in deep waters and looked for escape.

I looked for it in Nienburg's many cobblestone streets and lanes. The Saale river ran parallel to the town streets and I often sat on the bank and watched steamboats towing long lines of barges loaded with all kinds of cargo.

One day I saw fish in the river swimming upside down and fluttering their fins and flapping their tails in a most peculiar way. I saw lots of them, nice big ones, two or three kilos, so I ran and got Paul. We caught a bagful easily and I took my share home and put them in our bath. When Bertha, our cook, came to pull a couple out, they had recovered and were swimming right way up. Later, I heard the sugar factory in Bernburg had poured waste molasses into the river and it had fermented, making the fish quite drunk.

At home I had a collection of pet animals. I had angora rabbits, dormice, snakes, guinea pigs and tropical fish. I took care that all my pets were locked in their individual enclosures, but once, one of my snakes escaped and got into Mother's shop. I knew it was afraid and confused, slithering all over the place, behind boxes and under any cover it could find. One of Mother's best customers, Frau Schmidt caught a glimpse of my snake gliding about and screamed. I thought, 'How silly to be afraid of a non-toxic reptile'. I threw boxes aside and searched for it while Mother tried to calm the nearly hysterical Frau Schmidt. My snake escaped and flashed up the outside water pipe and when I rescued it, I put it under Frau Schmidt's nose to show her how harmless it was.

'Get rid of it!' Mother told me firmly. I never argued when Mother looked like that. As I returned my snake to its cage, I heard sounds of bright music coming from Hilde's room. It was a radio jazz broadcast from England. I asked Hilly if I could listen too, and I just loved it, it was so different from the classical music of Beethoven and Bach and Brahms.

As winter set in and it grew colder, every living room in town was cosy with coal fires. I liked to see the first snow falling lightly and softly through the double glass windows. When it lay thick enough, Paul and I took our sleds and spent hours sliding down the slopes past the public school to the bridge over the Bode River. Quite often, a friendly farmer would hook a whole line of our sleds together and tie them to the back of his horse and cart. What a grand ride we had, going up and over the Nienburg hills with the cold air nipping our cheeks.

I didn't look forward to summer so much. I had to work with Mother in her garden a little out of Nienburg. Every family who wished to grow fruit and vegetables had their garden plot, each one surrounded by a six-foot-high mesh wire fence. Mother had several dozen fruit trees, morello cherries and different varieties of apples and plums. With the help of Herr Seemann, a pensioner, she established asparagus beds and all sorts of salad vegetables. Black and red currant bushes and gooseberries lined the inside fence and along the outside fence, loganberries thrived. She beautified the garden with roses and beds of flowers. Colourful bushes surrounded a gazebo where we sat and drank cordial after our work was done. Mother knew a lot about gardening and planted horseradish outside the garden perimeter, knowing how quickly it spread and put down deep roots. One day she discovered an old man digging it out and throwing it into a heap.

Mother in her garden.

'What do you think you're doing?' exclaimed my astounded mother.

A smile lit up his old face. 'I'm giving you a helping hand, Frau Trappmann.'

Mother protested, 'Stop, stop! Don't pull my horseradish out, a fish dinner won't be the same without horseradish sauce!'

'Ah,' the old gentleman exclaimed, 'and I thought it was a weed.'

After school and at weekends, whenever the garden needed watering, Mother insisted I help carry buckets of water from a nearby pump—very heavy work for me. I refused to play sport at school, so I guess that was why Mother dragged me unwillingly to her garden. Several decades later I established a cherry orchard and the knowledge gained from working with Mother proved very useful. Another way to develop my undersized frame soon appeared when my friend Heinz took me along to the Boy Scouts.

The name of the Nienburg Scout troupe was *Pfadfinders* (the Pathfinders) and I enjoyed the good programme mapped out for us. Every weekend we went on long walking trips, sang German folk songs as we walked and slept in youth hostels. Pride in our country was very much part of the Boy Scouts movement. Our Scout leaders instructed us to respect and honour the soldiers, the national heroes who fought and died in the 1914–18 war. We laid flowers on the steps of the imposing Soldiers Memorial in Nienburg. That time of my life, as a Scout member, was full of youthful happiness, but it didn't last. I turned 13 in 1933, the year Adolph Hitler came to power and that changed everything. Heinz' father, who worked as a labourer in the cement factory and the flour mill, had the dubious honour of being the first Nazi party member in Nienburg and Heinz was very proud of him.

One night in 1933, when the Hitler Youth movement was only starting, two Hitler youth leaders came to the Boy Scouts meeting and immediately arrested our Boy Scouts leaders, telling us to go home and come back the next evening. Next night they lined us all up and announced, 'You are not Boy Scouts, you are the "Hitler Youth".' We were very surprised and one little kid said, 'We want our old leaders back,' but they ignored him. The national Hitler Youth leader, Baldur von Schirach, carried out Hitler's philosophy with great zeal. 'German

Youth shall be educated physically, intellectually and morally in the spirit of National Socialism,' he loudly proclaimed.

Under the 'Hitler Youth' banner, we carried on in much the same way for a while but then things changed. The camps were now run on military lines, our tents erected in straight rows. We were drilled strictly and taught how to march in order to become part of the army of the Third Reich. The camp commandant lectured us on obedience and duty, which he said would carry forward the glorious German military tradition. We learned pro-nationalist songs, our young voices singing of the invincibility of Germany. Our scout leader, Horst Webel, was always strongly patriotic, but after the Hitler Youth leadership training, he became something of a fanatic. He and others taught us anti-semitic songs and we ran through the streets of Nienburg singing, 'We'll hang all the Jews from all of the trees.' When I returned home, Mother was very angry.

'How could you sing that song, all of you!'

I was suddenly ashamed of being caught up in mob action of an odious kind and could not answer her properly. Mother's words indicated I was not in the right company. I thought about what the scouts had become. It was more than just nationalistic pride; it had turned into fanaticism. Not much more than a fortnight after that I quit. I just stopped turning up at the Hitler Youth meetings and it became the first of my desertions.

I could not tolerate a movement where I had to march around like a soldier but fortunately there was an alternative offered to boys who weren't active in the Hitler Youth. We were sent to school on Saturday mornings to learn about the pure Aryan race and Germany's great destiny under Hitler, our glorious Führer. For me, it was too dogmatic, too rigid and I didn't absorb any of it. My family background was anti-military—Mother's ancestors were shopkeepers and riverboat people,

Father's were musicians. This background did not help me later to fit easily into military training.

In Nienburg, it was traditional to celebrate the old festival days and Hitler made a point of emphasising the tradition of linking old German culture with modern times. A 'One Thousand Years' festival was held in 1934 and a carnival atmosphere reigned for a week. The whole town headed out onto the streets, with stalls set up around the town square, beneath acacia trees, offering high-class handmade goods of many kinds. There were rare treats like pineapples and bananas, exotic fruits only a few wealthy people could afford. We boys crowded round the stalls, buying chocolates and sweets.

The festival was a wonderful time for me. I rode on the carousel and popped into side show tents. Of great interest was the *zwitter* (half man, half woman) and I entered the tent, full of curiosity. 'She' stood in front of us, on a dais. A seemingly attractive woman in a pink dress and hat from under which dark eyes looked steadily at us, the gaping audience. Her name, she told us in a throaty voice was Henrietta. The sharp-eyed showman invited any doctor sitting among us to come up and examine Henrietta. Dr Summers, Hilde's doctor, was singled out but made no move.

'Don't be bashful, sir, Henrietta takes it all in her stride. Come along up, show people they're getting their money's worth.'

Dr Summers smilingly declined. 'Let her keep her secrets,' he murmured.

My friend Willie and I made for a beer cellar that was temporarily set up downstairs in the Council chambers. With magnificent aplomb, we stepped into the world of men and ordered a half-litre glass of beer each. We drank it down and climbed back up the steps, the world spinning around us. The solid figure of Herr Berner, our local policeman, confronted us.

'Boys, I hope you're not tiddly,' he said genially, quite unconcerned about our rosy cheeks and stumbling feet. I felt queer and said goodbye to Willie, weaving home with a light and airy feeling inside my head. Mother was out and Bertha set down my lunch but I felt strangely tired and tumbled straight onto my bed. When I awoke, the day was over and Mother refused to let me return to the festival. I had missed hours of fun and frolic but I felt there was some satisfaction in having moved a little closer to being really grown up.

Not too long after the festival finished, I was in the kitchen, helping myself to a sandwich, when Paul knocked at the back door with a big new rabbit in his arms. His father kept rabbits and killed one every so often for a family meal. The idea of keeping rabbits and providing a meal for our family appealed to my emerging sense of becoming an adult, so I joined the Rabbit Holders club.

Thirty male members met in a room at the Schiffchen Inn every month and talked so loudly and boastfully about their rabbits, the president often had to bang the table to bring them to order. Was it my imagination or did some of the members wiggle their ears and twitch their noses as they described the antics of their rabbits? The president was a bricklayer and spoke with such a funny lisp I wanted to laugh but dared not with his foxy eyes fixed right on me. As a kid I had enormous trouble controlling my mirth, it just burst out of me like water from a leaky pipe. I was the only young member among men, 20 to 50 years older and I knew the president would kick me out of the club if I didn't behave myself.

Soon after joining the club, I had acquired a variety of rabbits: white angoras, blue or white Viennese, Belgium giants and chinchillas. Herr Unger, one of our tenants, taught me how to make cages out of old timber boxes, with connecting doors and inner compartments. I fed my pets fresh vegetables and grass every day and Mother checked my cages for cleanliness and to make sure that I kept the straw clean in their cages.

Each year, club members grew excited about the Christmas Show when we entered our rabbits for exhibition. I won prizes for my angoras, carefully brushing their long white fur and presenting them spotlessly clean and looking beautiful. I built up my number of rabbits, as well as guinea pigs, and when I left home to start my apprenticeship as a pastry cook, I had 50 animals. I got a lot of pleasure from my furry friends; attending school was always an unwelcome interruption.

In secondary school, Herr Rektor Wagner, our teacher, put pressure on us to join the army. He was a Nazi and very intimidating, striding into the classroom, thumping his books down and demanding, 'Who is ready to join Hitler's army?' Half of the class stood up, so he continued, smacking his fists together, impatiently urging, 'Come on, come on, what's wrong with the rest of you?' Then another 25 per cent stood up, then everyone. I was the last, but I got up too, I didn't want to be black-marked and called a coward by my schoolmates.

I especially hated men like Herr Wagner, who were dedicated to army life and spoke about war as though it was the most marvellous thing. Dr Peter Haensch was another man in the same mould, he lived in one of Mother's flats and it was hard for me to dodge him. When he grabbed me, he'd shout, 'Germany needs boys like you for the army! Make your plans and prepare yourself to be a soldier! War makes men out of boys!'

I think my father's anti-militarist beliefs influenced the whole family, but I'm sure it was my own personal make-up which made me dislike the idea of joining the army. As far as I could see, the military didn't equip anyone for ordinary life at all, apart from training personnel in the use of radio communication. I had a special interest in radio and wanted to fiddle around with that sort of equipment myself.

I had a special aptitude for radio and made crystal sets at home, with good reception, and repaired Mother's radio and was pleased when she arranged for me to work at Herr Wiek's radio shop in the holidays. The day I started, one of Herr Wiek's workers was called out for a repair job and I accompanied him for experience. When we arrived the lady said she hadn't listened to the radio for a week. I was bursting with confidence and said to the tradesman, 'I bet it's only the fuse.'

He snapped, 'Shut up and be quiet, you know nothing about radios, I'm the tradesman!' He began working and spent an hour fiddling with her radio with me at his elbow.

I pestered him, 'Why not look at the fuse?'

He exploded. 'I'm doing this repair, you stupid kid!' After a long enough interval, he put a new fuse in and the radio worked. I felt very proud of myself, but was too young to think he might have deliberately created an hour's paid work for himself and his boss. I turned up next day and Herr Wiek didn't look pleased.

'Don't come any more,' he told me, 'You're not the right person to learn this trade.' That was how I didn't become a radio technician; I wasn't wise enough to keep my mouth shut.

I sought solace in the company of my lively sister Hilde. During this period of her life, I knew she had joined the Communist Party and was following the political trends with avid interest.

When the Reichstag went up in flames in 1933 and Joseph Goebbels immediately heaped blame on the Communists, she was incensed at this slur towards the Party. She declared it was one of Hitler's many acts of deceit to create a dramatic situation, inflame the people with his passionate hatred of Communism and reap the results for his own benefit. According to her, 'Anyone with any commonsense knew the mentally deficient Dutch Communist van der Lubbe was incapable of setting fire to such a huge brick structure'. Nonetheless, he was sacrificed for it. Together we listened to Radio London for the latest European news but the best pre-war news came from Radio France—its broadcasts were very anti-Nazi.

Hilde and I shared many common beliefs, the main one being our faith in Communism; together we listened to Moscow radio, convinced that the new society in Russia was the hope of the world and an inspiring example of the brotherhood of man. In 1930, Hilde had left school and obtained a job working at the *Volkswacht*, a liberal Social Democrat-orientated newspaper, run by a reputable publishing house in Bernburg. Straight after Hitler came to power, Nazis occupied the printing premises and took over its running, changing the name of the newspaper to *Trommler Verlag* (The Drummer). My sister and all the staff were sacked on the spot, the new management replacing them with Nazi supporters. Gestapo members began an investigation of all the former employees. They marched into Mother's house one morning, searching through my sister's library and all her belongings. But this was not enough, they searched the whole of Mother's large house from top to bottom and confiscated and burnt Hilde's extensive library of modern books.

Many books were taken out of circulation under Nazi rule, one of Hilde's favourites, *Jud Süß*, was written by Leon Feuchtwanger, a Jewish writer. This book was later made into a film, but was rewritten and distorted by a Nazi scriptwriter, who depicted the Jewish hero as a predatory rapist. Along with my sister's books and those owned by other people working at the printshop, the entire stock of books on sale at the publishing house was burnt. Freedom of thought was a thing of the past.

This persecution of my sister and the confiscation of her belongings was the beginning of my sympathy for the Left movement against Fascism. Later in my working life, I fully identified with its growing opposition to the Nazis' iron grip. We were the only ones in Mother's house who had a radio and although she was no supporter of Hitler, all her tenants were free to listen to his phlegmatic speeches. We had Nazi families living on the third floor of our home and one tenant listened intently to Hitler's every word, exclaiming, '*Sehr richtig*!' (Exactly right!). Because it was risky for us to listen to Radio London or broadcasts from France or Moscow, we closed all our doors and turned the volume down low. This 'crime' carried the penalty of death and we knew there were plenty of informers and SA men, or 'brownshirts', a paramilitary group that harassed Jewish people and protected officials at Nazi rallies, in Nienburg.

All Nazi members were SA men and every weekend they had their 'duties': dressing up in their brown shirts and marching for hours around the sports ground. They attended night-time 'thinking education' to keep them loyal to Nazi doctrine. On Hitler's birthday, every family in Nienburg fluttered a swastika flag in a prominent place at the front window. Once a year, SA men went to a big rally in Nurenburg to hear Hitler shrieking his racist supremacy theories. I stayed away from all the Nazi mass rallies, I had nothing in common with them.

In Nienburg, torchlight parades were organised through the main streets as evidence of support and loyalty to Hitler, with a turnout of SA, SS and Hitler Youth, along with the Bund Deutscher Mädel or BDM (The League of German Girls). The fire brigade band led the parade and everyone sang Nazi songs. As a member of the Hitler Youth, I carried a torch that smoked heavily and smelt of tar. In German tradition, the burning torch was a symbol of peace and freedom and Hitler incorporated this into public displays for his own despotic purposes. I must admit I enjoyed the excitement of this kind of activity and we Boy Scouts marched every weekend in what was called the gypsies park. In pre-Hitler day, gypsies had all the freedom to camp there, a right forbidden under Nazism.

Our town was by no means free of the sordid racist bigotry of Hitler's regime. In 1933, the gypsies, along with the Jews in our town were arrested by the Gestapo and sent to concentration camps. Some of my sister's Jewish colleagues disappeared and her good friend Fraulein Unger vanished. Jewish businesses were taken over by the Nazis, their slogans declaring, 'Don't buy goods from Jewish Shops, the Jews are our Enemies!' Another piece of Nazi propaganda was to blame the depression and mass unemployment following the war of 1914-18, on the Jews. During that dreadful night in German history, what the Nazis called *die Kristallnacht* ('the night of broken glass'), every Jewish shop had its windows broken and the stock pillaged.

Nienburg people learned about this horror through their local newspapers. *The Bernberg Drummer* newspaper boasted of the success of this appalling operation and the complete destruction of Jewish property. The Nazis' bellowed, 'The fight against the Jews is a just fight. The rage of the German people against the Jews is justified.' I knew that the Nazi's made up this line of racial nonsense, successfully seeking to enrich themselves at the expense of the rightful owners.

The Jewish Mendershausen brothers owned a flourishing granary in our town with five or six silos and a carrying capacity of a thousand tonnes in each. Heinrich was put in a concentration camp, but Erich managed to escape to America. Herr Hoppe, a Nazi, took over their granary. A Jewish owner of a textile shop, Herr Gotschalk, disappeared, presumably arrested and sent to one of the camps. Jews were not the only target of Nazi persecution, as a well-known Communist in Nienburg, Richard Fanselow, was arrested and sent to Dachau concentration camp.

All this greatly upset our family, we were not free to talk openly and express our concerns about what was occurring around us. Gone was a safe, reassuring atmosphere, politics were not discussed in cafes or pubs. The word *verboten* (forbidden) increasingly appeared in public places.

Lore, Mother, Hilde and I relaxing outdoors.

The majority of people living under Nazism succumbed to the constant beat of the Nazi drum. Nienburg's Bürgermeister (Mayor), Herr Schulz was a Social Democrat and at the 1933 annual ceremonial parade of the First World War veterans, made a zealously pro-Nazi speech. Hilde and I couldn't believe our ears—overnight he had switched his political allegiance to retain his position as Bürgermeister.

We, the German people, hailed Hitler as the new genius to cure all our nation's ills. In doing so, we allowed a democratic system of government to be utterly destroyed. Elections under Nazism were a farce as there were no candidates representing electorates. A voter was asked instead, 'Are you in favour of the Nazi regime?' Each polling booth had a number of books in which people recorded their votes by placing a tick beside the yes/no box on an open page. There was no secrecy, only people with no regard for their safety openly declare their opposition to the Fascist regime.

Even so, a courageous four per cent did register a protest vote. One of the main reasons for people's acceptance of Hitler was the memory of the deep depression when poverty stalked Germany and unemployment figures were at a devastating six million. This was the best breeding ground for Hitler to rise to power, and he got the credit for bringing Germany up out of the morass of poverty and deprivation.

MY HORIZONS WIDEN

At the end of my fourth form at secondary school in 1934, Mother turned up at the school and received a first-hand report from my teachers. I didn't relish Mother being there, it would hurt her to know the truth about my scholastic progress. I hadn't the slightest interest in history or English, I was O.K. in maths, good in physics and the study of nature. All practical things interested me. The headmaster sat her down in his office and said, 'Mrs Trappmann, your son will never be good enough in school, he wouldn't pass matriculation.'

Mother's pride was jolted as I knew it would be. 'School results are not everything. My daughter Hilde's reports were only average, yet today she can pick and choose her jobs,' she retorted defensively. 'She has worked in a variety of excellent jobs.' Her cheeks burned with love for us.

'Take Bruno out of school,' the headmaster advised my mother. 'Let him learn a trade, you're in a position to buy him a business.' Poor Mother agreed; with my unimpressive reports she had to.

My horizons widen

So, at just 14 years of age, I entered the world of everyday work. I began an apprenticeship as a pastry cook. I rode my bicycle to the little township of Köthen, 18 kilometres (11 miles) from Nienburg and met my future employer, Alfred Kettner, a restaurant owner and a top Nazi in Köthen. At first meeting, he looked reasonable enough: a bit skinny, straight dark hair and penetrating eyes. But after working for him for three years, I had reason to hate the Nazis. Frau Kettner was plump and spoke with loud authority, and when Herr Kettner left off bawling at me, she took over and had me running all over the kitchen. Over time, I worked out ways to even the score with them.

I started work at 7 a.m., first making a fire in the big, brick baking oven then, before breakfast, I rode off to the local dairy and bought all the milk and cream and cottage cheese the chef would need to turn out cakes for the customers or 'guests' as they were called. I had to mix and set the yeast dough in a big brown enamel pot and place it on a shelf in the oven and check it regularly to keep it at an even 30 degrees. Frau Kettner watched and checked on every movement I made, even at breakfast time while I was eating my two slices of bread with cheese and a bread roll spread with jam, she had her eye on the clock. I finished up with a cup of leftover coffee from the night before. I felt hungry a lot of the time; nothing seemed to fill me and I scraped out cake bowls and dishes for scraps. I was growing fast, making up for the years when I was undersized.

I had a bed in a room upstairs. It had one big shabby chair and a sharp-cornered cumbersome wardrobe. The walls were covered with ancient plaster. The glass in one small window was grimy with age and kept the early morning sun out. It didn't matter how unpleasant the room was, I was too tired to notice anything, just tumbled into bed and fell dead asleep, thankful to rejuvenate my exhausted body.

The boss stayed in bed until dinnertime, recovering from his late nights. Weekends, he was up till 1 or 2 a.m., keeping the restaurant open, and his wife came down early and took charge of everything.

I worked alongside Paul, the tall, good-looking chef, a single man of 25. He turned out mouth-watering cheesecakes, black forest cakes, bee stings (a dough-based cake with a honey, butter and almond mix on top) and many other varieties the boss sold in the restaurant throughout the day and evening. I liked Paul, he didn't boss me, nor did the waiter who came on mid-afternoon and worked till midnight.

Most of my work was washing dishes and cleaning and scrubbing the floors and benches. Everything had to be spotless or the boss would begin roaring, flashing his cold, green, deep-set eyes everywhere. I was glad to get on my bicycle, to deliver cakes and drinks to private houses for this or that house party. I had a basket between the handlebars and a little trailer fitted behind the bike. One day, when a ferocious dog came running out at me, snarling and barking, I got such a fright I spilled all the cakes on the ground, damaging most of them. I thought of throwing them over a hedge and telling the boss I delivered them. But I decided to take them back to the restaurant and show Paul in the hope that he had some spares.

I went in with my basket and there was the boss, drinking a cup of coffee. He saw the damaged cakes and his face turned an unhealthy red. 'You stupid kid!' he yelled, jumping up, tottering backwards and running at me, slapping both my cheeks. When he was prancing about in a rage, I became quite adept at ducking out of his way. This was part of teaching me the trade and making me submit to him, but he had no hope.

While he ranted and raved, I held my breath and stared at him without blinking. The veins stood out on his ridged forehead and thick neck as he exploded violently against me. I looked with interest at his lips as they collected flecks of cream spit. When he had done ranting, worn out with passion, I went and stealthily stuffed myself with his best marzipan. I had to even the balance a bit in my favour—I was working from daylight until dark and getting nothing for it.

I guess I had been spoilt all my life. With two sisters and two aunts, I never had to wash a dish, let alone scrub and clean from morning until night. I had been petted and protected and, to a degree, pampered. Now I was learning how other people lived.

Every evening in the restaurant, Kettner and his wife served the public guests with a wide variety of wines, beer and spirits. He gave me a key and instructed me to go down to the locked cellar and bring up whatever he wanted. He showed me how to take the bung from a new keg of beer and connect it up.

When I served the customers in the restaurant, I wore a uniform, pants and shirt with black and white squares and a white cap. I guess I looked a sight and I felt stupid wearing it; I was not fully grown and the clothes hung on me. The mirror showed my face, fresh and smooth, no facial hair as yet and my head was topped with thick, light brown hair. The lady customers were especially nice to me, probably because they had sons of my age. I looked forward to seeing my own mother on my afternoon off every two weeks. I left at 2 p.m. Sunday and returned at 7 a.m. Monday morning. I treasured those hours of liberation. I complained to Mother about my job.

'I'm a slave, I get worked to death!' She didn't sympathise.

'You're a learner, you have to put up with it.'

On Sunday afternoon, to make the most of my few precious hours of freedom, my friend Paul and I walked to the Forest Rest Inn. There was gay music and dancing and people of all ages romped about like youngsters. I drank in the frivolity and I drank a lot of beer as well and forgot my grievances. In the evening, Paul and I went to the Spring Hotel close to home. I had an insatiable appetite and from the pub's menu I ordered raw minced steak flavoured with onions and spices. This was a very popular dish and after several helpings of it, plus a bockwürst, I felt fortified enough to go back to the sweathouse. Next morning, at 5 a.m., I was on my way, cycling the 18 kilometres (11 miles) to Köthen.

Lore, Mother and me, the young apprentice.

As part of my pastry cook apprenticeship, I was to learn cake decoration. Kettner was stingy and had unheard-of ways of saving money. He refused to buy kitchen paper. When I needed a paper funnel to squeeze cream onto a cake, I had to make it out of newspaper. He would instruct me to scrape the cream off the newsprint. Rather than discard the inky cream, Kettner would tell Paul to colour it with dye. Paul wouldn't do it, he just threw the contaminated cream in the fire when the boss went out.

I could never satisfy the boss, he was always complaining about the appearance of the kitchen. 'Look at the state of this floor, the place looks like a pig yard! Get down and scrub it properly.' My levels of revenge would reach new heights. I would grab a dozen eggs, make holes in the end of each and drink all 12 of them, then I scrubbed the floor.

In 1936, when German troops occupied the Rhineland, Hitler made a triumphant speech and the papers were full of it. I was uneasy because I thought our troops going in there would bring the prospect of war closer but Kettner was elated, he threw a big party in his coffee lounge for his Nazi colleagues, and beer and schnapps flowed like water. One of Kettner's Nazi guests began telling me how great a man 'our beloved Führer' was. He had watched a parade and seen Hitler at close range.

'I was disappointed,' he told me, 'he was wearing make-up! Imagine, a great leader like that, he doesn't need to wear make-up!'

It didn't matter to me what Hitler put on his face, he could get painted up like Punch and Judy for all I cared. What did matter was building up our armed forces. Where would it all end?

An important event happened that year—our country hosted the Olympic Games. They were held in Berlin and hailed as a great success. The only trouble was that a non-Aryan, Jesse James a black American, was the outstanding athlete of the games, winning four gold medals in his events. Herr Kettner did not celebrate this. It must have been too much of a blow for Hitler, seeing a sportsman from an 'inferior' race win against 'pure' Aryan stock. He left the stadium before the games were finished. Inwardly I was laughing, but to my boss it was no laughing matter. He applauded Hitler's walk off, 'Why should our great leader lower himself and give gold medals to a nigger!'

Being a true Nazi, Kettner was a racist, which was reason enough to loathe the man. He wasn't a happy man and his discontent with the world spilled over onto me. In his eyes, I was a failure. 'You're no good for nothing, you'll never be able to make it in this trade or any other!' He never tried to stand over Paul, he was a good cook and besides he was a lot bigger than the boss, but my ears and cheeks often burned under Kettner's heavy hand. He gave me an excellent reason to hate all Nazis.

In Nienburg, the Nazis took the first of May, traditionally our Labour Day, and made a great salutation to Hitler out of it. One day, when Kettner was being particularly objectionable, I hopped on my bike and rode straight to the union office and complained about him to the trade union secretary. I thought he was sympathetic, for he said, 'Alright, I'll do something about him.' Feeling very satisfied with myself, I rode back to work.

Immediately, the boss pounced on me.

'Where have you been?' I stuttered some excuse and his face went red.

'Don't lie! If you've got complaints, tell me, instead of sneaking off and telling somebody else. I cannot tolerate undiscipline and disobedience!' His mouth was working with rage. 'You lazy, witless, no-good, you know nothing about our great nation! There are no class divisions under our great Führer, no middle or upper class, only the workers with the fist and the brain.' He gave me a hefty push. 'Get back to work and try to use what little brain you have got!'

At the end of my apprenticeship, three and a half years of what I regarded as slaving among cooking pots, the examiners from the Cake Makers Association arrived from all over Anhalt (our small state) to test me, to decide if I was skilled enough to receive my certificate as a pastry cook. They began by asking me political questions. 'Where was Hitler born?' one examiner fired at me.

Another asked, 'When did he come to power?' And, 'What do you think about Stalin?'

I knew what was expected, so I said, 'Stalin is a *bluthund* 'a blood hound'. I felt ashamed, but I was forced to keep my true feelings to myself. After they finished, the president Herr Muschmann said he was very happy with my performance and shook my hand.

'You passed with flying colours. Pick up your certificate at four o'clock today.' I was there right on the dot and Herr Muschmann appeared but I was surprised to see his hands were empty.

He said, 'Sorry, Bruno, we have to send your certificate. You will receive it by post in a couple of days.'

When my certificate did not arrive, I began thinking of a possible reason. Several weeks previously I had been in the restaurant, serving guests. There was not much business, so I sat down and wrote a letter to Mother. As I wrote, many grievances came into my mind. I told her that on Saturdays I had to work as late as two in the morning, cleaning big oven baking trays and all the large heavy basins sticky with dough and every other dish in the place. All the cutlery had to be shining and spotless. In other words, I had two jobs; one was learning the trade, the other was a cleaning drudge.

'Mother,' I wrote, 'I can't put up with it any more, I'm happy my time is soon over.'

In the middle of writing, some guests arrived and I got up to serve them, leaving my letter on the table. Soon it was closing time and I was glad to stumble upstairs to bed. I began to undress when I remembered my letter. Quickly I ran downstairs. I could hear Frau Kettner's voice, she was reading my letter to her husband. I knew I was in trouble but I opened the door and confronted them.

'I left my letter in here.'

'Frau Kettner looked down her nose at me and said haughtily, 'There's no letter here!'

Herr Kettner's eyes glittered with malice. He stiffened his back and stood over me and growled, 'I'll deal with you tomorrow.'

I went to bed wondering what Kettner's revenge would be. The chef Paul and I shared the same room and when he arrived home from the pub, I told him what happened and he thought it was a great joke. A week later my certificate arrived, the examiners had given me the lowest possible pass. Obviously Kettner, as a high-ranking Nazi, had blackened my character and ruined my chances with the examination board. I was disillusioned with the whole cake-making business. I resolved when I finished with Kettner, I would never again work in the pastry trade.

A CAREER CHANGE

When I finished my apprenticeship in 1937, I worked for Mother as her store manager, buying stock for her shop, studying all the trade papers and making contacts with suppliers in Leipzig and Berlin. Her business was going well, Hitler had turned Germany into a prosperous country, jobs were plentiful, the massive unemployment of the early thirties had gone and everybody had money. But we Communists knew the cost of Hitler's leadership in terms of human misery.

I travelled about and enjoyed my new job, buying cutlery, manchester, haberdashery and selecting ladies dresses and accessories. Once I struck a deal with the manager of a big firm, buying a package of miscellaneous goods for 400 dollars. Included was a wide range of articles in knitwear, assorted clothing, underwear, sewing materials and many other items I didn't bother to check. I delivered the goods to Mother, imagining myself a smart businessman able to handle a profitable transaction. But Mother discovered among her new purchases some undesirable items.

'Bruno! You're a sheep! Look what you've bought! I can't sell these things in my shop, these ... these preservatives!'

She threw a package at my feet containing 200 French letters. I felt a real fool and learned never to buy bulk packages again. After a year in the commercial world, I felt like a change. I wanted for nothing materially but my goal was independence.

At this stage of my life, I had plenty to say to my friends, but my growing interest in girls made me awkward and self-conscious. I was 17 when Mother advertised for a housemaid and several young girls came to the shop looking for work. One of them was absolutely lovely and I said to myself, 'That's the girl I want!' Her name was Charlotte, she was from Koethen, and Mother hired her as a kitchen hand and for general house cleaning. I fell dizzily in love with her. Weeks went by before I had the courage to ask her out and when she agreed, I was absolutely overjoyed and proud to have this beautiful young girl on my arm in public. Mother gave me freedom to go to social functions, usually to a licensed cafe or inn—there was no such thing as under-age drinking in Germany.

Charlotte and I set off with another couple to go to a dance, walking one or two kilometres to a forest inn where the dance was held. Young couples did not have far to go to make love under the forest trees but I was convinced Charlotte was not that type of girl. Love for her put my mind in a whirl, I stumbled around in a daze, only happy when I could see her and catch her up in our passageway and kiss and cuddle her. When she returned my kisses willingly, my pleasure was complete. Charlotte had a bedroom next to mine, connected by a door Mother had expeditiously blocked by a huge wardrobe. As time passed, I began thinking Charlotte might permit me to enter her room. One day, I asked would she like me to push the wardrobe aside. She drew her breath in with shock and surprise, but her eyes were bright with laughter. After Mother and my sisters retired for the night, I carefully and without a sound, moved the wardrobe away from the door. As I stepped into her room, Charlotte lay giggling under her bedclothes. I felt very nervous, although I loved Charlotte, I had no experience and no idea how to make love to her. But she was helpful and whispered things in my ear and I was delighted and proud with myself. I loved Charlotte more and more and felt my life could not be more wonderful, our love-making was all the sweeter for it being clandestine.

Suddenly my rosy bubble burst when my friend, Helmut Seger, who lived near us, one day took me aside, looking self-satisfied and mysterious. He told me Charlotte was bestowing sexual favours on him. My heart hammered in my chest, 'You're making it up,' I said hotly.

'It's true and she goes out with soldiers from the anti-aircraft defence as well. Ask her, she'll tell you!' My world turned upside down, I felt cruelly deceived and my self-pride received a terrible blow. How could she do this, I asked myself miserably. That night, with a heavy heart, I pushed the wardrobe back into place. Not long after that, Charlotte began going out with a dashing young tugboat skipper with dark eyes and black hair. He had the job of towing a line of loaded barges down our Saale River.

Charlotte threw up her job with Mother and spent a whole week away down the river with the young skipper. My disillusionment was complete; if all girls were like Charlotte, I wanted nothing to do with them.

One day I met Wolf, a young worker from the Nienburg cement factory, an irreverent youth, always ready to laugh at Nazi activities.

He declared, '*Für jeden forz ein fackelzug*!' (For every fart, we've got a march).

He was right—Nazi members organised marches through the town for special events like Hitler's birthday. We had a march to open a new bridge in Bernburg. Every May Day there was a march and Hitler used this traditional workers' day to celebrate his Nazi party's power over them. At night, there would be torchlight marches led by a top-ranking Nazi and three bands. After meeting Wolf, I decided I wanted a job like his among ordinary, working-class people.

I had the choice of working at the cement factory or on river boats and I couldn't decide which one to take. One night in a small pub I met Otto Sager, a man in his late twenties, an anti-fascist and a free thinker. Otto played the violin in Nienburg pubs for pure pleasure and although married, enjoyed social life like a single man. When war broke out he was part of an anti-aircraft crew and shot down British and American planes coming over to bomb strategic targets. I told him I was looking for a job and he advised me to see Dr Ritter, an industrial chemist at the cement factory.

'It's an easy job, you can sleep all night and bring home 35 marks each week.'

Otto wanted to make big money and had a dream to track down a Stradivarius or a similar priceless violin and sell it. He knew Mother had my father's two Guadagninis, very valuable Italian instruments, and tried very hard to buy them, using all his persuasive powers on Mother.

'Mr Sager, I'm not selling them,' she told him firmly. 'I don't need the money.'

Otto was not rebuffed, grinning cheerfully and casting his roving eye on my sister Lore. She quickly put him off, scorning a man who could be unfaithful to his wife.

I was granted an interview with Dr Ritter, who controlled the cement-making in all three factories in the town. He scrutinised me for a long minute before informing me there was a vacancy at Jesar-Bruch, the oldest of the three.

A career change

I quickly accepted the job but, before starting, I made over Mother's garden. I created curved garden beds with tilted brick borders and built a fountain and fish ponds with water plants and waterlilies of different colours. I stocked the ponds with macrodes and small fish from the Saale River and caught salamanders from wild swamps and added them to the pond life. I bought a couple of non-venomous snakes, native to Germany, and let them loose in the garden. Mother's appreciation was the seal on my satisfaction.

Me with my wonderful sisters.

I Deserted Hitler

It was 1938, my 18th year, when I began work at Jesar-Bruch. My job was to collect samples of the cement in its early stages from huge containers and take them to the laboratory for analysis. I liked my workmates, a lot of them were mature, middle-aged men who made no secret of their hatred for the Nazi system or their belief in Communism. My sister Hilde had aroused my interest and I looked forward to learning more from these men. They could clearly sense the drift to war, they knew Hitler had given orders to treble the size of the army and were shocked but not surprised when in March 1938, our Nazi troops overran Austria. In November of the same year, troops invaded Czechoslovakia and these old Communists were exasperated with Neville Chamberlain who allowed himself to be duped by Hitler at Munich.

When the Nazis took the newspaper *Trommler Verlag* (The Drummer) over and gave Hilde the sack for her Leftist beliefs, she found a new job in Magdeburg, working in the Polte munitions factory. But she had tired of that and started working as a draftswoman in Junkers aeroplane factory in Bernburg. Junkers vast industrial plant so impressed her with its size and importance that she forgot her allegiance to Communism and became a Nazi adherent. She lodged with a dedicated Nazi woman living in Bernburg. Before eating breakfast they clicked heels, saluted and shouted 'Heil Hitler'. Not many gave the Nazi salute with clicking heels and rigid arms held at forty-five degrees, but Hilde's landlady's salute was perfect. She worshipped the Führer.

I was astounded at Hilly's switch of allegiance and told my Communist friends at the cement factory about her. 'She's been seduced by Nazi power,' one told me and I understood what he meant. All the Nazi bands, flags, uniforms, spectacular parades and marches, all the mass cheering and excitement was a fabulous unfolding epic to my live-wire sister. Some Communists were fascinated with the grand rituals, and although disavowing Hitler's outpourings of hate, they attended some of his Nuremberg rallies purely to observe the mass intoxication and fervour of the hundreds of thousands who drank in his words like wine. I stayed away—I had nothing in common with Hitler worshippers.

One of the men I had to see every hour on the job was Otto Fricke, a lime miller, a typical working-class man. Otto was particularly incensed about the treatment of the Jews.

'They've got no rights,' he told me. 'The Nazis have stripped them of German citizenship and hounded them out of shops. No bakers or butchers or grocers are allowed to serve them and they can't get medicines from chemists! You mark my words, Bruno, the rest of the world is watching us and we'll never live down what's being done to the Jews!' I felt the same disgust as Otto did at the treatment of the Jews.

Otto's son was my age and I visited him and his father many times at their home. Frau Fricke was a nice woman and made me feel at ease. We listened to radio broadcasts from Luxemburg, London and Moscow. I had many long talks with my friends at the factory on night shift, when it was safe to talk, out of earshot of the one Nazi among us, a big fat electrician. I remember one lad coming into the laboratory and lifting his arm up in the Hitler salute.

'Look,' he said, laughing, 'That's how high the shit is in Hitler's Reich!' The night shift was easy and I often took along the piano accordion I purchased after hearing Will Glahé play. Will was a virtuoso and a great favourite with young and old, drawing large crowds to cafes in Berlin and other towns. I played mine half the night and forgot about taking samples of cement, nevertheless the cement was first class, quite often the men took half a bag home on their bicycle handles.

I played the accordian for many years. My stubby fingers couldn't play the
violin, but they could manage the accordian just fine.

Before I left for work one morning, I heard news on the radio that Hitler ordered our Panzer divisions into Poland. And this was what threw the whole world into the second bloodbath of the century.

A career change

On 2 September, one day before my 19th birthday, England and France declared war on Germany. At work, all of us knew we would be plucked out of our jobs and conscripted for the army, no matter whether we supported Hitler or not. We were in for full-scale war, triggered by Hitler's lust for power. I was the youngest among them and I was drafted first.

REICH'S WORK DUTY

In the winter of 1940, I, and a lot of my school friends, were forced to join *Reichsarbeitsdienst* or RAD (Reich Labour Service), a six-month period of military training. We were paid 25 cents per day and later, when we transferred to the army, it was increased to 50 cents as danger money. After several months training in the Harz Mountains, using spades in lieu of weapons, we were transported first to Belgium, then to Holland and France.

We began digging airstrips to fabricate authentic runways and from the air they looked like the real thing.

Our lieutenant told us, 'Work fast, don't be fussy.'

Big machines were called for, but spades were our only tools and our only weapons—in fact, our one important possession. We cleaned them and printed our names on them. We marched with them, worked with them and drilled with them over our shoulders. We even slept with them!

In January 1940, I had some leave from the RAD and went home to join the family. One Sunday morning, we were having a leisurely breakfast when a knock sounded at the door. Our maid ushered in a very pregnant young girl who shyly asked to see Mother. The girl was one of the Polish workers forced into Germany to do factory work and other menial jobs. Mother knew she had no clothes for her baby so she quickly got up and went into her shop, returning soon with a huge parcel for the girl.

After she left, I asked Mother, 'Why did you do that?'

Mother said, 'She is Polish, she is poor and has nothing.'

I felt a warm glow of pride—why couldn't everyone be like my mother and treat people living on the other side of national borders with sympathy and understanding. But Hitler's racism didn't allow tolerance; the Polish people were a race he regarded as far below his Aryan ideal.

My leave was soon up and back I went into training. The war was going victoriously for our Panzer columns with one success after another, it seemed they were invincible. It was *blitzkrieg* alright! Hitler wanted to conquer England and terrorise the British, so he ordered raids against their cities and towns. I listened to Radio London and could understand what those people were suffering.

When British planes began intercepting our Luftwaffe aircraft, Hitler was furious. He frothed and fumed and vowed over the radio that the Luftwaffe would obliterate every city and town in England. He ranted about Britain being our main enemy and was set on sending over an invading force. I heard Churchill's speeches over Radio London, putting heart into the British people and I regarded him as a great war leader. Right through the war I wanted the Allies to win because of my deep-seated hatred for Hitler and Nazism. In May 1940, the English forces were driven out of France and had to be evacuated from the coast at Dunkirk. Paris was threatened by our armoured divisions and victory for the Allies seemed a long way off.

In Belgium, we were occupied unloading munitions from railway trucks and sending them to the Front in France. The people running pubs and restaurants gave us young soldiers a jubilant welcome; thousands of soldiers meant an enormous boost to their trade. In the Netherlands, we were just as popular. For a rollicking good time we went to Rotterdam, it was off limits, but we went just the same. Everything we wanted was there: schnapps, beer, dancing music, girls and the best fried fish in the world. We lived each hour to the full, singing, drinking, toasting any of the fresh-faced Dutch girls whose attention we could capture. We sang to them:

> *AnnaMarie*
> *To go away from you hurts*
> *Because I love you so much*
> *I give you the good-bye kiss*

I guess I must have overdone it a bit because the army police came in and arrested me and I paid for my self-indulgence with three days in gaol. Shortly afterwards, in June 1940, we were ordered into France to do work behind the lines.

One day, our Red Cross sergeant called me in saying, 'Arbeitsmann Trappmann, I am making you the Red Cross orderly for our company.' He gave me a Red Cross band to wear on my arm but I didn't feel up to the job and I had no special training. I had a tent full of sick soldiers to look after with colds, flu and other minor complaints and with the rain continuing, I knew there would be plenty more.

During manoeuvres from one town to another, our heavy trucks got bogged in the soft mud, the unmade roads were so bad. Our sergeant ordered a few of us to hang onto the back of a bogged truck to give it more weight and prevent it sliding deeper into the mud. Some of the young fellows were skylarking around as the driver of another truck connected chains to pull it out. As the tow chain tightened, the truck gave a lurch and one of the young lads lost his grip and fell under the wheel. He had no time to save himself—the wheel just ran over him, crushing his chest. I waved frantically for the driver to stop but it was too late, the young soldier lay there unconscious and coated with mud.

I felt heavily the weight of my ignorance; I had only a vague idea of what to do if my comrade was still alive. I could feel no reassuring beat from his pulse and had a feeling nothing could be done for him. He made a few feeble movements, then lay still. His open eyes stared unseeingly at his mates standing around, silent and shocked. The stamp of death on his young face was something I had not seen. It was tragic, he was so young, barely 18 years of age. His parents no doubt would have accepted their son's death fighting the enemy but here he was, killed under the wheels of our own army vehicle. Later, as I learned from personal experience, it was not always the enemy who killed our soldiers.

Hitler was turning his attention to the invasion of England, code named, 'Operation Sea Lion'. From Rotterdam, a fleet of invading ships were being equipped to take our troops to the English coast. Our corporal introduced us to 'our' boat, commandeered from its owner for the invasion, a big rusty iron ship, so old its name was unreadable. Formerly, it had been a coal transport vessel, now it was covered with dirt and rust, a 'floating coffin' some of us called it. More likely a 'sinking coffin'! We were marched on board and a closer inspection did nothing to reassure us. I got goose bumps looking it over. So did my mates when we learned we would be packed into a deep hold under the decks on the day of the invasion. I was convinced this old ship would never make it across the English Channel and I couldn't help making some remarks about the stupidity of this war.

'You talk like a Russian Commissar,' one of my comrades said, looking hard at me, thinking I might be a Russian spy.

Thankfully, we were saved from a watery grave when Hitler lost the 'Battle of Britain' and changed his plans to invade the country. Very soon our RAD days were over and all of us were sent home for three months.

In Nienburg, I found everyone in good spirits. Germany was on top, with one military victory after another, the little countries succumbing to the military might of the Third Reich. My home leave came to an abrupt end in January 1941, when I received a telegram stating, 'Report to army headquarters at Sondershausen.'

The training at Sondershausen was rigorous, we were drilled and marched unmercifully. I hated doing the goosestep, to me it epitomised Nazi military control and my spirit rebelled. I never mastered it and my legs shot out at amazing angles. My mates laughed and our corporal ridiculed me.

I had become good friends with Gerd Bargles, a well educated youth with a middle-class background. He had a very cultured voice, addressing me as, 'Bruno, ol' boy.'

What drew me to him was his opposition to Nazism, he was dead against it, but like all of us he had no choice. When on leave together, headed to various pubs, he made straight for a piano and played jazz. The top brass decided he was officer material, but he didn't show much respect for authority. When the sergeant bawled at us and gave us extra fatigue duties, Gerd swore, 'I'll have him sharpening my pencils when I am an officer.'

When we finished at Sondershausen, we were ordered to Erfurt to regroup as an army unit. Gone were our familiar spades, now we had rifles and were decked out in dull green uniforms and steel helmets. I was becoming more deeply immersed in military life, which would ultimately deliver me to the battle zones, but I did not have much opportunity to feel disturbed about this.

I was in a scouting division under General Heinz Guderian's control. The general was known for developing armoured warfare and from Erfurt we advanced east, crossing over the Polish border and camping on the outskirts of Warsaw. While we were in this city, I saw the Jewish ghetto sprawling over a huge area, taking up a whole suburb, its high walls topped with barbed wire. Open streets were blocked by soldiers patrolling to and fro, and nobody other than army guards could go in or out.

Gerd and I visited a Polish family living next to our camp. Gerd had his eye on the daughter and I talked politics with the father, an educated man.

'I know why you Germans are here,' he said. 'Any day now you'll be marching into Russia.'

Our officers had told us we were bound for Africa but, of course, we didn't believe that nonsense, nor did we believe there would be a war with Russia. Germany had signed a non-aggression pact with that country, but there were sceptics among us.

Over Berlin radio, Hitler screamed a tirade of hate against the Soviet Union, declaring Stalin was hungry for other territories and little countries like Latvia and Finland needed the power of Germany to conquer Stalin's strategies. On 22 June, we were ordered to advance over the border to Brest-Litovsk and found ourselves in Russian territory. It had all happened so quickly and I realised what lay behind Hitler's tactical move in signing a peace treaty with Stalin. Caught off guard, not expecting an attack from the West, the Soviet Union would fall into his hands.

ON THE ROAD TO MOSCOW

In mid-summer 1941, a few months before my 21st birthday, I was on the Russian Front, participating unwillingly in Hitler's Barbarossa, code name for his attack on the Soviet Union. My pacifist beliefs made war abhorrent to me; never did I want to serve in an army, I am not a disciplined person and my character rebels against army discipline. But there I was, thrust into combat with all the other German youths of military age without the luxury of having a choice. Our enemy was Communist Russia.

I was very concerned about this. Deep in my heart, I had sympathy for Stalin because I believed him to be a great Communist ruling over a more equitable society.

I discovered my mate Gerd Bargles thought the same way as I. We were both against authority, both against our armies driving deep into Russia. Apart from our belief that the Soviet Union was not threatening Germany, there was Napoleon's humiliating defeat in Russia all those years ago, to show that it would not be easy to take over this great Communist power. We treated Hitler's idea that Germany was peopled by a superior race as a joke and jokes of that sort among my close companions helped keep our spirits up.

I was in General Guderian's 21st Army, in the motorised infantry section. I wrote to my sister Lore and told her I was part of the Investigation Division. It had three mobile sections, small tanks, motorbikes with sidecars and trucks. I wrote and said how much I wanted to be in the section with small tanks. 'Then I can wear a smart black uniform no girl can resist.'

She wrote back and said, 'Don't worry about the uniform, worry about what the Bible tells us, "Thou shalt not kill".' My sister's words struck home and I thought, 'She's right!' I resolved never to kill anyone, but what could I do, caught in the army noose? At my swearing-in ceremony, we all had to repeat the words, 'We swear by God that we are obedient to the Führer and the Fatherland.' I had substituted the word 'pot' for the word 'God'. I hadn't had the chance to talk things over with Mother who was a free thinker. I could sense her concern for me but she saw there was no way out for me to dodge the army.

I wrote to Lore, 'Did you know all of us have inscribed on our belts, *Gott mit uns* (God with us)? How can God bless us if we have guns in our hands?'

She replied, 'This God on your belts is not God, it's the Devil.'

And Hitler was my idea of a living devil, driving Germany deeper into war, making enemies of peaceful neighbouring countries. He was determined to have *Lebensraum* (living space). I could not agree with his avowal that Germany needed more space to dominate Europe. Colonisation of another people's land was a denial of their independence and human rights. Africa was for the Africans and Russia for the Russians. Our dealings with other countries should be an exchange of goods in a free and open market without war. I could agree with nothing of Hitler's philosophy.

But we marched steadily onwards and for the first time in my life I stood on Russian soil. It was momentous! It had that look too, wide expanses of land, so flat it could go on forever without end. I regretted being part of the army invading it, advancing swiftly and deeply into Russian territory, passing villages at the rate of 100 kilometres (62 miles) a day. The dwellings looked primitive but solid, made of stone with roofs of straw. The smallest of windows made the interiors dim but no doubt practical to keep out the cold.

In the first days, our motorised infantry division moved forward with trucks and motorbikes. Gerd, as the motorcycle pillion rider, carried a machine gun and I was in a sidecar, armed also. It didn't take our officers long to realise Russia was not the country for motorised vehicles. The roads were impossibly rough, having never been levelled by machinery or topped with metal. Trucks had to carry loads of equipment but the infantry advanced on foot, encountering only small enemy resistance. We advanced through village after village and rarely saw young men, only women and children and aged people. Young men had vanished, presumably into the Red Army. Already Hitler was predicting the end of Soviet resistance, his speeches ringing with triumph. We soldiers believed him and many times over we saw Russian soldiers retreating, so it seemed they were already beaten, not having the military strength to withstand our mechanised panzer divisions. As we advanced further, I could see Russia had beautiful vegetation and forests of birch trees, giving the country its real character. We saw blueberry bushes and picked what we could and ate them with relish.

One day our Corporal said to us, 'The Russians have abandoned a truck, who can drive a truck?' Straightaway I volunteered and became one of the transport drivers belonging to the rearguard transport, driving over the rutted and uneven roads. I carried supplies of uniforms and various other goods. I had the company's tailor sitting next to me in the cabin, a small skinny man, and by the look of him, a born pessimist. He was in charge of all the replacement uniforms and boots.

Many events remain in my memory of our trek into the Soviet Union. One morning, after an enemy night raid on the village where we were camped, a driver came up to me and told me his truck had been burnt. 'Come over and help me salvage what we can.' We unloaded supplies of milk chocolate flavoured with coffee, tinned meat and rye biscuits. Another time, I had to transport the body of our *Oberfeldwebel* (senior sergeant). We were in a convoy of trucks and motorbikes, advancing east towards Smolensk when suddenly a Russian plane zoomed low over us, its machine guns firing, killing our sergeant instantly. My truck was closest and he was lifted and put on the back, there was no opportunity to bury him, we were on a forward push and the poor fellow lay in my truck for three days with biscuits and other food supplies. In wartime, hygiene did not exist.

As our company marched towards Minsk from the south, we saw a dozen Russian tanks, T-34s, bearing down the road towards us. The Russians made these tanks so solid our ammunition bounced off them. We leapt off the road and began digging holes anywhere for some sort of cover; our rifles were useless. The next thing I knew, a soldier next to me jumped up with a grenade in his hand. He threw it, trying to knock out the first tank. He was shot instantly. My young mate looked at me with horror.

'Bruno,' he panted, 'Is that your brains all over you?'

'It can't be,' I said stupidly, looking at the thick splatter covering my tunic. Then I saw the young private lying on the ground, his head blown away. The tanks continued on down the road. I don't know why the tank crew didn't kill the lot of us, but I had the feeling the crew in the T-34 had a more important mission than blowing our heads off.

When the tanks were out of sight, we dug our poor hero a soldier's grave at the side of the road. We marked his grave with a cross made out of birch wood. Later, after this hopeless act of bravery, he was awarded a posthumous decoration. Everyone who served in the winter campaign in Russia received a medal. We called it *Gefrierfleischorden* (The Order of the Frozen Meat). I collected mine later in hospital, together with another for being wounded at the Front. The third time I was wounded, the army sergeant told me to apply for another one, the Golden Wounded Medal, but I didn't fill in the papers, it was against my principles. I believed a pacifist should not have medals for war service on his chest.

Time passed so quickly while we were fighting that, at one stage, I realised we had only been in Russia for two weeks. So much had happened in that short amount of time, my life before the war seemed years away. I had been on guard duty all day and that night I was woken by my mate coming into our tent after his two hours on watch. He said to the sergeant, 'I've got a Russian prisoner, he's a deserter, he's come over from the enemy lines with his hands up. What do you want me to do with him?'

Without hesitation, the sergeant replied, 'Shoot him!' I lay still with all my nerves tingling. A couple of minutes later, I heard a shot. I lay there shocked. I was flooded with relief that I had not been on watch duty. I knew I couldn't have shot an unarmed man in cold blood. My friend had no choice. If he had refused to carry out the sergeant's order and shoot the prisoner, he would also have been shot. I felt so out of place, there was no room on the Russian front for soldiers with pacifist ideals. I did not know how I would survive the war. I was locked into a grim game of war where individuals didn't count and forces bigger than myself would determine the outcome for me.

On the road to Moscow

From Minsk we advanced to Smolensk, which fell to our Panzer divisions in July 1941. Our section encountered tough Russian resistance in a small coppice, but Guderian's strategy of encircling Red Army troops was giving us easy victories over them. With each engagement, thousands of Russian soldiers were trapped by this strategy, our generals were using superior military tactics and were able to overrun a less experienced enemy.

But some of our officers acted like fools, believing in the superiority and invincibility of the German race. They positioned themselves in the front line in full uniform, medals glinting in the sun, their shining buckles and buttons on the distinctive uniforms making them a target for the Russians. They encouraged us, urging us on, our young colonel shouting a war cry, '*Tataratar*!' (forward). Not unexpectedly, he and three other officers were shot, as well as other soldiers. When we knew more new young officers were being flown in from Germany, we nudged each other, 'More cannon fodder!'

After the victorious motorised advance on Smolensk, we buried our dead officers and soldiers. The prisoners we captured had uniforms fit for the Russian climate, rough and ill fitting, made out of yellow-brownish, inferior-looking material. I was shocked to discover they were armed with rifles made by the big industrialists, Krupp and Mauser (the same Krupp family my father used to play for), not as modern as the ones we had but bullets fired at us were German bullets shot from German guns trained on us through sights made by Zeis, a well-known German manufacturer. What is the sense in all this, I wondered. Here was Germany trading off weapons designed to kill soldiers of the Fatherland. That surely meant that we, the front line troops, were disposable, just so many commodities in the game of war. Had I not been a Communist already, seeing the German brand on the prisoners' guns would have made me one. My disenchantment grew, I was not willing to be shot for Hitler to realise his grand plan of expansion into Russia's vast territory.

As the Russian resistance to our forward march became stubborn and tough, I kept back, strategically positioning myself at the rear of the line. I was not alone. Some officers displayed a healthy survival instinct. Herr Von Alvensleben, an aristocrat with the rank of a lieutenant was at the rear with me, keeping out of the firing line. I found it rather funny that an officer whose grandfather, Gustav Alvensleben, was a general in the Prussian army, shared my lack of commitment to soldiering. His ancestors' castle was in Gatersleben. Later, after the war, I picked Hallimasch mushrooms with my young wife on his family's estate. By then it was under Russian control and open to the public.

As Russian resistance tapered off, giving us a few days to recover before the next engagement, a truck driver brought over a package of music records.

'Have a look through these,' he said, 'See if they're any good.' They were part of the now-dead colonel's belongings. I flipped through them, American jazz hits from the thirties, 'Tiger Rag', 'Alexander's Ragtime Band', 'A-tisket, A-tasket' and others.

I showed them to Bargles and his eyes glistened. Like a lot of middle-class Germans, he enjoyed listening to jazz in the privacy of his home, away from the cold eyes of the Gestapo. As I handled the records, I thought of the young colonel buried under Russian soil. I could see him plainly: tall, healthy, a great athlete, a sportsman, head and shoulders above the rest of us. When we came to a watercourse, he was first over, his long legs leaping it with ease. I never knew, never suspected he played music emanating from black musicians; especially as he was the one out front, urging us forward, indoctrinated by master race theories.

Someone found a record player and we had many cheerful sessions going through the treasure trove of records. I loved the jazz tunes and was soon playing them on my piano accordion. For me, jazz was a true symbol of freedom devoid of any strict martial beat and full of joyful tunes, the complete opposite to the heavy, ponderous strains of Wagner's symphonies that Hitler recommended to all of us Germans. For a brief magical interlude, music took us straight out of the battlefield into normal life. But it wasn't to last. Our next thrust forward was towards Orol. The speed of our advance left little time to do other than follow orders and try to stay alive.

As we charged further eastward, the Russian people were silent and passive as we passed through one after another of their villages. Although we were well stocked with provisions, as we penetrated deeper into Russia, our soldiers were free to raid peasant property.

A dozen of us, plus our corporal, took accommodation one night in a poor, two-room dwelling. One room was for the young woman inhabitant, the other for her cow. The young woman was poorly dressed in what seemed to me to be just rags. She had no stockings or footwear, her feet were swathed in old material tied around her feet. It was clear to me that the cow was her only possession and, when our corporal decided to kill the cow and produced a big knife, she gave a sharp cry, rushed to her cow and put her arms around it, making desperate gestures to show him the cow had a calf. Her appeal had no effect on our corporal. In peacetime he was a family butcher and quickly killed the animal, slicing it up while the woman, bent low in a corner of her hovel, wept for her cow and unborn calf.

The corporal cooked it in the young woman's oven and we sat down and ate it with a good appetite. She ate some too, her body overcoming her mind's objections. I sensed her feelings and felt ill at ease, wishing myself many kilometres away from her tear-filled eyes. How she must have hated us, the invading army, as we marched into villages as conquerors, taking over their lives. And I was part of it, far from my home and everything I knew and loved, because of the fanatical will of a dictator us Germans had put into power.

Much of what I saw in Russia upset me. As we advanced forward from village to village, we slept on the earth floors of Russian dwellings and lived with Russian families. Peasants stood quietly as we moved in, they knew they had to put up with us. On one occasion we were in a dwelling occupied by a proud, old Jewish couple. I tried hard to make friends with them, but they looked at me with distrust. The Nazi persecution of Jews had spread fast. I offered them rye biscuits and other food but they would take nothing from me, a German soldier. I read the hostility in their eyes. How could they know I was in their land against my will, that I was against what the Nazis were doing to Jews everywhere in Europe.

One night, we were woken up with a shout. 'Everybody up, the enemy's coming! Leave the village, *schnell, schnell* (quick, quick)!' The enemy used the tactic of attacking by night, a good time to inflict maximum damage on us. In my haste, I couldn't get my truck started, so I retreated on foot with the rest. The sergeant major was incensed.

'Soldier Trappmann, where is your truck?' My explanation was not good enough. 'You will be prosecuted!' he thundered. My truck went back into Russian hands so once more I was a foot soldier.

I was lucky to have one or two good mates, who thought as I did but the majority of the spirit among our soldiers was strongly pro-Hitler, pro-Nazi and pro-Fatherland. I could hardly find anyone who was convinced that military invasion by Germany was wrong. The dozen soldiers in our group were convinced that Germany would be the absolute victor in this war—we had over three million men on a 480–kilometre (300-mile) front and our panzer armies were the best mechanised force in the world. It was not unlikely that we would be home by Christmas. As the Red Army began to counter-attack, this spirit of optimism underwent a change. We felt the Russian soldier's stubborn resistance; he was fighting for his Motherland, the land that nurtured him. However primitive, it was his homeland.

I was disappointed about the backward living conditions of the Russian people, particularly in the small villages. I had expected the Communist philosophy of equality for all to have included the peasants we encountered on our journey. Instead, the villages had no lighting, no sanitation and no running water. The women carried buckets of water into the dwelling on each end of a rough yoke, drawing water from a hole dug in the ground and framed with wood. The whole family slept on the big oven top, which kept them warm at night. They provided themselves with a nocturnal supply of sunflower seeds, chewing the seed and spitting the husk out like parrots.

Having done my apprenticeship as a cake maker, I was very interested in the oven, which dominated almost an entire wall in the small Russian abodes. It was built from stone and sat on the earth floor. The top was covered with layers of heavy stone and thick clay, rendering the surface smooth and level for the family's slumber. I heartily approved of this oven; no matter how rough and primitive, it was constructed exactly right to bake food to perfection.

In the morning, the mothers rose first and mixed and kneaded a great mound of sour dough made of coarse rye flour and potatoes. The bread was dark and heavy, probably very satisfying and nourishing, but we soldiers didn't fancy it. The women were built solidly for their burden of work. The only males in the villages were old men, other able-bodied family members were away fighting. The women and children were poorly clothed, no one wore socks or stockings, just rags tied around their legs and old wooden-soled shoes on their feet. The mothers wore scarves covering their hair. I could see the peasants lived a life far removed from the standard we took for granted.

Moving around Europe as young novice soldiers in the RAD, we had experience how other people lived. In Holland, everything was spotless, the Belgian and French people were far less particular, but compared to these, Russia was centuries behind all of them, life here was back in the Middle Ages.

THE RUSSIAN WINTER
CLOSES IN

In Autumn 1941, when we were close to Smolensk, heavy rain fell on us and straight away we discovered the unpleasant fact that Russian roads were not serviceable for a mechanised army in wet weather. Soldiers, horses, tanks and mechanised vehicles struggled through swampy woodlands and muddy roads. Conditions worsened and our advance was laboriously slow—the heavy artillery, trucks and tanks ended up stuck in the mud. As winter clamped down on us, all of our German armies were immobilised; Mother Russia supplied the Red Army with its most effective weapon, it was simply MUD!

General Guderian planned for the German troops to reach Moscow quickly, achieving a strategic and moral victory. This never happened—we were stopped 40 kilometres (25 miles) from Moscow with the weather turning against us. It began to snow heavily and we experienced our first real trials in this vast unknown land. When we tried to advance, it was unsuccessful against stiffening Russian resistance and we suffered as they bombarded our flanks with heavy artillery.

We were caught unprepared for the harsh wintry conditions. Everybody from the generals down had been convinced the war would be won before the Russian winter arrived. Hitler was making the same mistake as Napoleon; he was stepping into the French general's footprints, deep in snow. His determination that Moscow must be taken, no matter the cost, no matter how fiercely it was defended, had landed us in this predicament. Napoleon couldn't conquer Russia with his armies on foot and Hitler wasn't doing any better with all his mechanised might. The idea that we would have the war won and be home for Christmas in the same year was now a joke.

I was glad to receive welcome letters from home for Christmas, together with a package Mother sent full of homemade cakes I shared with my mates. What made me even happier was a warm sweater she hand-knitted for me. I was used to cold winters but in Russia the temperature dropped to below 40 degrees. We soldiers were too lightly clad for these temperatures, our accommodation in poor Russian dwellings provided us with warmth and shelter but bugs and lice came out of the cracks in the walls and it was difficult to sleep with them making a meal of us. I got rid of the lice in my shirt by hanging it out in the freezing air. Next morning, they were still clinging to my shirt, frozen stiff.

One frozen morning I walked out of the dwelling where some of us slept to relieve myself, and when I came back, one of my mates said, 'Bruno take a look at your nose in a mirror.' I saw a white spot covering the end of my nose. He warned, 'Don't touch it ... it'll fall off!' Ten minutes later when I warmed up, the frozen white spot disappeared. From the intense cold, our beards and woollen balaclavas covering our chins were frozen stiff. We tried to protect ourselves from frostbite, but were hampered by wind, snow and sub-zero temperatures. By now, our army division was 20 kilometres (12½ miles) east of Orol in the depths of winter.

I was part of the advance lookout squad in the early months of 1942. We were loaded onto a sled pulled by a small, strong Russian breed of horse and taken to the outpost where we took up our positions. Most peasants owned a horse and sled, a practical and necessary mode of transport in these conditions, so our army commandeered these items for our own purposes. After several trips to the front, the horses knew the way even though thick snow covered the ground and all identification marks were lost. We tried reaching our posts on foot in the beginning, but only ended up walking in a big circle. One day we saw a wolf watching us from 100 metres (109 yards) away so we were very glad of those tough little horses, they offered us some protection and their instincts to find the way in that vast snowy terrain never failed us. No matter how thick the fog, how dark the night, how dense the snowstorm, they got us there.

WOUNDED

In the middle of winter 1941–42, we encountered heavy enemy resistance 50 kilometres (31 miles) south of Moscow. It was my eighth month in Russian territory, and Russian troops were using heavy field guns on us, plus fire from their infantry. I was shot in open country while on lookout duty with my mate. All night the Russians had pounded us with artillery fire and, as it grew light, our corporal roused us to a full alert emergency. I took my position at one of the lookout machine gun posts set 100 metres (109 yards) apart. We were close to the outskirts of a village near Mtsensk and suddenly I saw something strange coming towards us. I strained my eyes trying to identify it. Against the lightening sky it looked like a line of dark trees that had the strange ability to move towards us. As it came closer to us, I saw it was a dense line of Russian soldiers advancing steadily, elbow to elbow. I was afraid; my heart was pounding. I thought for certain it was the end for all of us. There were so many coming at us but my mind was set against shooting any of them.

Wounded

We got the order to open fire with our machine guns and I slanted my gun at an angle above their heads and pulled the trigger. Instead of a burst of rapid fire, my gun fired a single shot and when I tried again, another single shot. Because the temperature was so far below zero, my gun had frozen up. Then I heard a great stirring behind our line as back-up troops from the village came running forward, shooting at the enemy. I didn't look around, I was too engrossed watching the Russians coming closer.

All at once I was struck from behind, knocked over by a shot. I cried out and my nearest mate came running and picked me up. We forced our way through the thick push of troops charging forwards, running over the top of us, blind to everything but the enemy. I was worried about my wound and then a second, stronger feeling flooded me. This would get me out of the front line alive.

I was taken to the Red Cross station and I immediately saw I was not the only wounded solider; another mate of mine had a wound in his stomach and was moaning in great pain. The next person I saw was our corporal, a good man and very close to all of us men under his command. He had been shot in the head and was gabbling unintelligibly, shouting scraps of words, louder and wilder every minute, waving his arms, it was shocking to see him like this. Medical orderlies tried to calm him and give him treatment, but suddenly he fell forward with not another sound and was gone.

My wound was dressed and I was taken to the temporary hospital set up in a building in Orechovo, 50 kilometres (31 miles) south of Moscow.

I was crawling with lice when I arrived at the hospital and the medical staff decontaminated me. The wound in my arm wasn't serious. In the pre-battle confusion, I had been shot by one of our own men, the flesh wound clearly showed the direction the bullet. After a week, I was discharged and I found myself a place to stay with an old Russian mother. This was strictly against army rules, but I had some thinking to do.

I reported back to the hospital daily and collected my rations from the army canteen issued to soldiers absent from their company. The longer I was away from the front, the less I wanted to go back. Qualities that made a man a good soldier were entirely lacking in me and I was not alone in this. Heinz, another soldier, had turned up after walking away from his company and was just drifting. I felt sorry for him, knowing his fate if he were caught.

A few days later I fell ill and my temperature went up so I reported to the same doctor who had dressed my arm. His face was like red granite. 'You're back again!' he shouted, 'Get back to the front, there's nothing wrong with you. I'll report you as a malingerer!'

'Herr Doctor, there's something wrong, I've got lumps all over me.' He glared and ordered me to undress.

One glance at my belly was enough. 'You've got spotted typhus,' he pronounced. I had acquired this disease from being bitten by lice. It wasn't good news. A lot of my fellow soliders contracted pneumonia as a complication from typhus and died. I was sent to a quarantine hospital in Bransk and spent three weeks there recovering.

While there, I received a tremendous shock when reading the local field army newspaper. The military police had caught a deserter and I instinctively knew without any doubt it was my friend Heinz. For his desertion, he was sentenced to death and hung by the military authorities.

I laid the paper down, shattered by the news. It brought home to me how very close the execution squad was to a deserter! Typhus had saved me from sharing poor Heinz's fate. I thought of the risks tomorrow held for me, but dismissed the thought. Life was precious and I was alive. Then, I found out I was ordered back to Germany for further treatment at a hospital in Zelle.

Wounded

In the train, on the way to Zelle, I became good friends with a Russian called Joseph, a young man in his mid-20s, also heading to hospital admission. He worked as an interpreter for the German military staff and wore a German uniform. He was heavily built and resembled Joe Stalin—dark eyes, prominent nose, his hair thick like a dark brush. His family lineage dated back to many past generations in Germany and I was certain he was Jewish. We had some good discussions about the theory of Communism and whether its application in his country had given the people a better standard of living. I told him I had seen the primitive little dwelling places without a hint of any conveniences for the people. He was highly intelligent and very well read and pointed out how far back Russia had started from and how far Russia had advanced since the days of serfdom under the Russian czar.

After we were settled in at the hospital, he transferred all of his belongings to the bed next to mine and our friendship carried us through the boredom of hospital life. We talked politics all day, but were careful—any anti-Nazi views would have brought us both to the gallows. He told me the German invasion was a surprise for all Russians, not even Stalin had expected the attack, even the presence of so many German troops in Poland had not alerted the Russians.

Joseph was having trouble with his eyesight and was issued with a pair of spectacles and I felt anxious as he looked much more Jewish wearing them. I confessed my doubts and said, 'Do you need to wear those glasses, Joseph?'

He shrugged and said, 'I'm useful to the Germans, I'll be O.K.' Alas! His optimism was misplaced. I was sent home to recuperate and during that time I wrote letters to Joseph and sent him a dozen tins of Mother's blackcurrants picked from her garden.

It was great to be home to see Mother and my sisters. Her business was going well. In 1938, Hilde had been briefly married but left her husband the day after the wedding. Six months later, she decided to have a baby and the man she chose was Adolph Weissgerber, a Bernberg man, who she worked with at the Junkers factory.

I never met Adolph but he must have been very presentable for Hilde to choose him. She kept on working after she conceived and gave birth to a full-term baby, a boy she named Peter. She gave little Peter to Mother to look after and went back to work at another branch of Junkers, this time in Fritzlar.

Hilde told me no Russian slaves were used at Junkers but she had heard most of the big industries used large numbers of them. This Junkers factory was close to a huge dam and I got news through Radio London that the British air force burst it open one night using a special type of bouncing bomb.

It was a great victory for the British, but a disaster for the people of Fritzlar when the dam broke and flooded their town. Hilde was incensed and told me the human cost of this bombing. She regarded the British dam busters as cold-blooded criminals and was haunted by the crying and screaming of the drowning people as they fought for life in the black floodwaters. I saw it as another of those horrible acts of war in which innocent victims are sacrificed.

My leave seemed to pass in a flash with the Russian front looming nearer on my horizon. One early morning, a week before I was due to report back for duty at the military centre, there was a loud hammering at Mother's front door. An army corporal stood there with a pistol on his belt.

'Get your uniform on immediately. You're coming with me.' I tried to get my thoughts in order as I dressed, trying not to think of poor Heinz and hoping his fate would not be mine.

On the way to the camp, I ventured to say to the corporal, 'I understood I had another week's leave.'

'We need people for the front line,' he barked.

I felt relieved; the army had more use for me alive than dangling at the end of a rope. The corporal escorted me back to the large army centre where I was trained and up to the third floor of one of the imposing brick buildings on site. I was ushered into the presence of a large army officer who exuded military authority. He gave me a hard stare and consulted some papers in front of him. My fears returned, did he have a record of my days of freedom away from my company?

He asked sharply, 'Do you know why I sent my corporal to pick you up?'

'Yes, Herr Major, the corporal told me you need soldiers for the front.'

He smiled ironically. 'Think about another reason. Does the name Joseph mean anything to you?'

'Yes, Herr Major. He was my best friend in the hospital in Zelle.'

'Do you know he's a Jew?'

'I had not the slightest idea, Herr Major.'

'You wrote him letters and you sent him food. Why did you associate with him?'

'He was in the bed next to mine, Herr Major. He had no relatives in Germany and no friends and I wanted to take him home with me for holidays.'

'What did you talk about? Did you talk politics with him?'

'No, Herr Major.' I began to feel confident I would survive the major's interrogation. 'I did crosswords with him.'

'Did you know he was a spy?'

'Of course not, Herr Major.'

'Well he is. He will be shot.' The officer closed the file in front of him. 'You can go now, I can see you're not involved in anything suspicious.' He fixed his hard eyes on mine. 'Just remember, Jews are scum, no fit German would spit on them.'

I left the building and walked quickly to the nearest pub, my mind seething with unrest. I had to immediately find a telephone! I knew very well Joseph was not a spy, but I had written a letter to him, an incriminating letter that would damn me and some of my dearest friends, the Fricke family. I had given the letter to Otto Fricke's son who was in the army stationed in Bergen where Joseph was. In the letter, I told Joseph to trust the bearer of the letter. 'He is a good friend, a Communist from a good Communist family, you can talk openly to him.' I was sweating, what would be the consequences of my unthinking remarks? Most likely the whole Fricke family would be rounded up and arrested.

My heart was beating hard as I heard Mrs Fricke's voice over the phone. 'Did your son leave this morning for Bergen?'

'Yes, Bruno, why do you ask?'

The next words were hard to utter, I had to admit the danger I had placed her family in. 'Mrs Fricke, I gave him a letter, did he leave with it?'

'No, Bruno.' There was a pause. 'I had a feeling about that letter, I opened it and burned it.'

'Oh! Thank heavens you did!' A great millstone fell from my neck. Like many Germans hostile to the Nazi regime, Mrs Fricke had developed a sixth sense to protect herself and her family from the traps that lay everywhere. I could feel the top-heavy power of Nazism over us all. I bought myself a congratulatory beer and as I hastened back to the camp, my feelings of euphoria lent wings to my feet. I did not know it then, but in a matter of days I would be sent straight to the Stalingrad front. Before I left, I received back the tins of blackcurrants I had sent to Joseph. It hit me hard but it was obvious the Nazis had done away with him.

AT STALINGRAD

Early in 1942, I received orders to rejoin my old company. I joined up with other soldiers, like me, bound for the Stalingrad front and boarded a train, which took us straight to Taganrog on the Sea of Azov. It was a long journey with the unchanging scenery of the Russian steppe ever before our eyes, a lot of it covered with vast crops of wheat and I realised I was looking at the source of Eastern Europe's 'bread basket' now within reach of Hitler's grasping hand.

We had what I thought was a welcome change when the train ground to a stop in a tunnel for us to relieve ourselves but how devastatingly wrong I was! There, before my eyes, was an unforgettable sight. The whole tunnel was full of human excrement and the stench was overwhelming, there was no clear place to put my foot down. My mind grappled with what lay before me until I realised I was looking at a scene of mass human tragedy, one of prolonged human suffering and privation. A trainload of captives, destined for a concentration camp, had been held there for days in trucks, like cattle. I quickly got back on the train, my mind full of the horror and suffering of those people. I could not dismiss them from my mind. How could I fight for a regime that was committing such awful crimes?

When we arrived at Taganrog, the peasants were selling huge juicy melons in the open markets, banana melons and watermelons. 'What are those tall hills?' I asked, gazing around me. Someone said, 'They're not hills, they're sand dunes.' I was intrigued, so I climbed up and saw a wonderful sight—a huge stretch of water, so extensive I could not see any land on the opposite side. I was looking at the Sea of Azov. Growing up in Germany, where we only had rivers, this sea was something new and fascinating. It was a hot day in mid-summer when we arrived and we quickly dropped our army gear, took our uniforms off and dived in the warm water, so clear we could see the clean sand on the bottom. One of my friends broke the surface, holding up an object.

'Look what I got! *Ein seepferdchen*! (a sea horse).' I took it from him and examined this minute and wonderous little creature, the first one I had seen and I couldn't help but marvel at nature's diversity.

After the refreshing swim and a rest, we marched 60 kilometres (37 miles) to Rostov, then we boarded army trucks to take us over the Don river and on to Stalingrad, 500 kilometres (310 miles) away. Wheat crops gave way to bone-dry land, the exposed earth a greyish colour covered with patches of coarse grass extending to the unbroken horizon. On the long trip I didn't see a single Russian or German soldier, nothing stirred, I could have been looking at a peaceful country not one embroiled in a major war.

The further we travelled the more I knew we could never win this war—the lines of communication were too long, the vastness of Russia was against us. Another major transport difficulty was the train line gauge in Russia. The train line was wider than the gauge in

Germany, so German rail trucks were useless on Russian lines. German engineers changed the gauge as far as Taganog, but it was slow, hard work. Rails were torn up and replaced and it was impossible for the work to be done all the way to Stalingrad. Relief trucks, transports and other supplies took too long to reach the battle zones. All our military might was concentrated on far-flung Stalingrad and both Hitler and Stalin knew this was the ultimate struggle, both were determined their armies would be victorious. It did not take a military strategist to know that with our German front line so drawn out, we could easily be circled from behind and cut off and that is just what the Red Army did at Stalingrad.

On rejoining my company, I discovered a lot of my friends were missing, killed or wounded. Those who had survived this long were given a low rank as a boost to their morale. Two weeks later our company was camped on the hills west of Stalingrad. I looked down on the picturesque, tranquil city, an unforgettable sight with the beautiful Volga River gracefully winding through green banks and tall trees.

Songs of the Volga were stored in my memory, particularly one from Franz Lehar's opera entitled, '*Es Steht Ein Soldat am Volga Strand*' (There stands a Soldier on the Volga Bank). I remembered a Russian song, a real old Russian melody about Russian serfs dragging river vessels from the Volga banks, using large ropes. With its catchy tune, the song was popular around the world in its English-language version 'The Carnival is Over'. Another song was 'Volga Schiffer' (Song of the Volga Boatmen). As soldiers, we sang our own words to it, '*Unrasiert und fern der Heimat*' (We are unshaven and far from home). Any other time I would have taken great delight in the peaceful scene laid out before me, but I felt only deep regret. Stalingrad would be under imminent heavy attack from our Sixth Army of 300,000 men under General Friedrich Paulus' command.

My company camped for a week in a thick forest of birch trees west of the city, preparing for the momentous battle. It was enjoyable, warm sunny weather, but our Stukas kept up dive-bombing attacks on the city below and utterly destroyed the tranquillity. During this time of marshalling our forces, a thought kept occurring to me: why not shoot myself instead of waiting for an enemy bullet?

The order came for us to advance and we launched forward on foot, going steadily down a gully backed by artillery positioned above us. Suddenly there was a blast in my ears from a grenade exploding close behind me and I felt grenade splinters penetrate my arms and buttocks. A medical orderly grabbed me and half-dragged, half-carried me to a medical post. We passed an officer on a field telephone and although rather stunned by the explosion I registered his rage, complaining and bawling into the mouthpiece that the artillery range was too short. 'It's falling among our own troops!' So that was it—I had been once again been wounded by 'friendly' fire.

Along with other wounded men, I was put in a Junkers air troop transport to return to Germany. It was a risky flight—Russian anti-aircraft gun fire exploded all around the plane and I thought any minute it could be the end of us all, but luckily our plane got through to Dnepropetrovsk and I was delivered to a temporary hospital bed where I was assessed as a non-serious case. When I settled in, I wrote to Mother and told her where the grenade splinters had lodged. One of my mates, looking over my shoulder, said with a laugh, 'Tell her you were shot in both cheeks but your face is O.K.'

Mother wrote and told me, while I was away Hilde had had another baby, a daughter called Maxamillian. 'Hilde is living at home with us so she can be close to her children.' Life went on without you when you were in the army.

Hilde with her children, Maximillian and Peter.

Next, we were put on a train to Lipstadt in Germany, a town of 15,000 people. On the trip I developed hepatitis. My eyeballs were yellow, my urine brown and when the train reached Germany, I could see people on the platform staring at my strange, dull-yellow skin. I was admitted to Lipstadt hospital, a small Catholic hospital run by friendly nuns. The sergeant in charge was also very friendly—too friendly! I had to restrain his hand groping under my bedclothes! Twice a week an army doctor inspected us, some were very sick and in the following weeks many died around me. One poor, deluded soul was delirious and raving, proclaiming out of his dry, caked lips, 'Victory will be ours'. Very soon there was silence from his bed. I was one of the lucky ones. After treatment and special diet, the yellow tone faded from my eyes and skin but it took me three months to fully recover from the illness.

I Deserted Hitler

During that time, the sergeant in charge issued us with passes to go and enjoy ourselves at dances and pubs. From his remarks, it was clear he was against the war, and with every passing week, it became clearer that Germany would not win it. Stalingrad was holding out against us and I heard over Radio London that there was bitter street fighting in that city and I was thankful to be out of it. One very important factor, which led to us losing the war, was the Red Army's dogged determination not to surrender their strategic city, no matter what the cost.

One day, our friendly sergeant told us the Doctor General in charge of all army hospitals was making a visit the next day to find men to send back to the front. 'Better go to the pub for the day, don't come back till six o'clock,' he advised us. 'Us' was a group of avid anti-Nazis—Gunter Lages, a Communist, Fritz, a vicar, myself and a few others. I had a lot in common with Gunter, he was a strong, handsome fellow with hazelnut brown hair. Our outlook on life was similar, we shared common tastes in music but the most important thing we agreed on was politics—he was strongly anti-Nazi. We talked politics openly in the ward and none of the other soldiers offered any opposition to us.

We went to the pub in a group, feeling highly elated at this unexpected chance to enjoy ourselves. We pushed some tables together and invited girls to join us. Our vicar professed no interest in girls, but I noticed his fingers slyly pinching a plump female bottom or two. He was about 20, just through theological school when he was drafted into the army as a simple soldier. He was slim with thin brown hair and grey eyes sparkling with fun, his serious thoughts only emerging when politics were discussed. He was totally against everything Hitler stood for and he supported the concept of a Communist society even though he did not talk openly of this. One afternoon we noticed two Dutchmen sitting together, obviously spies watching and listening to us, so we made up some incredible stories for their twitching ears. For a short time during these enjoyable sessions at the pub, the war didn't matter.

One night, listening to Radio London in the ward, we heard that a thousand British aircraft had bombed Cologne, civilians paying the heavy price of Hitler's obsession with power. Now with Britain's mastery of the air, German cities were suffering what Coventry and other British cities had endured. More and more, this war was becoming a war where civilians had no immunity against their nations' enemies.

I had taken the precaution against being sent back to the front by binding my arm in a sling to make it stiff and weak. The splinters of grenade were still in my arm and my buttocks and when I was admitted to a surgical hospital in Lipstadt to have the splinters removed, the corporal in charge of the ward administration woke up to my plan. He grabbed my arm, ripped the binding off and forcibly straightened it.

'You fraud,' he roared, his face red with rage, 'I'll bring you to the Army court, they'll get you!' I had a few bad nights sleep over that, but no-one turned up to arrest me. A surgeon dug out the splinters under my skin and I was transferred back to the friendly Catholic hospital.

In one of our good times at the Lipstadt pubs, I met a young Yugoslav girl from Bosnia. She was very young, 16 and pretty, with shining dark hair and dark glowing eyes, her southern European features giving her face a spellbinding character. I was starved for female companions, their lyrical voices and soft beauty were heavenly to me after so much male company. I saw Annie twice a week and fell in love with her, courting her for two months under the hawk-like eye of her mother, Matilda, who acted as a constant chaperone. Matilda dominated her daughter's life, but I didn't let her heavy presence put me off. I asked Annie to marry me but this was not possible until she became a German citizen. For that reason, she had to leave and go to Lodz in Poland. She said a tearful goodbye, knowing we would be separated for six weeks. In the meantime, I was discharged from hospital and went home on leave.

When six weeks had elapsed, I travelled to Poland, picked up Annie and brought her home as my future wife. To Mother, Annie was a great disappointment. Annie came from a poor household in Bosnia. Mother was no snob, but she wanted me to marry someone with a good education, someone she could appreciate and talk to. She was convinced Annie and her mother just wanted to catch an eligible young German for security, for a safe home in Germany away from the war. Between the two, I guess the disenchantment was mutual. Annie was very upset when Mother passed her off as a servant to our wealthy cousin from Magdeburg.

During this time I was not home, I was back in the army, training in the middle of the Harz Mountains in central Germany. I had given Annie my photo and she placed it on the bed table in her room, but according to Annie, Mother had whisked it away. Shortly after, my fiancée packed up and left what must have been a very disagreeable atmosphere. But I had more urgent things to worry about as I was sent from the Harz Mountains back to the Russian Front.

I SHOOT MYSELF

In the middle of the freezing Russian winter of 1943, news came that General Paulus and his Sixth Army had surrendered at Stalingrad. Hitler was consumed with rage, denouncing Paulus as a traitor to the Fatherland. He had expected the General and his men to fight the Russians to the last man, no matter what appalling conditions they suffered. I remember Hitler, in one of his tirades, proclaiming there was no such thing as surrender for a German soldier. His words were interpreted as, 'Wherever the German soldier stands, no other soldier will ever be allowed to put his foot.'

Only one-third of the vast Sixth Army survived and I imagined the suffering endured by our troops, trapped in the city with General Manstein's forces from the north unable to rescue them. Hitler led us, the youth of Germany, into an awful bloody dance!

On my way to the front, I found new mates and soon discovered there was a new feeling of disenchantment among them, they talked about shooting each other as a way out of the war. I thought yes, that's it, why wait until I get shot? A transport officer clearly understood the feelings among us and said, 'I have to deliver you back at the front, but I'll tell you this. The quickest way you can get home is by an ambulance train.' My friend Adolph and I got together and conspired to wound each other, but we had to watch and wait for the right opportunity.

Russian and German armies faced each other near Mtsensk and I experienced my second encounter with 'rasputitsa', the season of rain and mud in Russia. The roads were impossible, our tanks and other vehicles were continuously stuck in deep mud. In the first battle, Adolph was wounded and taken out of the line, so I had to make other plans. In the meantime, with survival my main prompt, I began moving slowly backwards … backwards. I was not the only one moving backwards and a very young officer, a major, saw us and bellowed. 'Don't move backwards or I'll shoot the lot of you!' Soon after, the whole German front was moving backwards under the impact of a heavy Russian offensive.

One day I was beside a soldier named Anton who was convinced we should be fighting the Russians, not retreating, but I could see he had no stomach for fighting, 'I'm sick of it,' he confessed, 'I want to go home.' I talked to him and after a while I suggested we make a plan to shoot each other. For a moment he looked horrified, it was against his commitment to fight for the Third Reich, then his survival instincts rose to the surface and he nodded. We made a plan and talked over how best to carry it through. We left our posts several nights later and began walking westward as quickly as we could. We covered about 10 or 20 kilometres (12½ miles) back from the front line without seeing anyone, then an artillery company spotted us. We said we were lost so they picked us up and brought us to Orol, a lovely place, but perhaps it seemed lovelier away from the battle zones.

We got our bearings and found our way to an army cafeteria and had a good meal. We spent some relaxed hours there, eating and dozing off, then suddenly I could feel someone's attention focused on me and aroused myself immediately, ready for action. Then I burst out laughing, there was my old mate Fritz, the vicar. 'It is you, Bruno!' he exclaimed. 'What are you doing here?' When I told him we had deserted and planned to shoot each other, he showed no surprise. 'Come and stay with my troop for a while, you're welcome! We've got a temporary house here in Orol.' Fritz and his company were having a short spell on their way to the front line and I was delighted to meet him again—the weather was fine and the countryside peaceful. We talked a lot, Fritz and I, there was complete trust between us. Of my desertion, he was completely non-judgemental.

I took up his friendly offer for Anton and I to stay with him for three or four days. The next day one of Fritz' mates couldn't find his cigarette lighter, and straight away, he blamed Anton. 'You took my lighter! Get your bloody boots off!' And there it was, in Anton's left boot.

I apologised profusely to Fritz and told him we would leave straight away. Some way down the road, I said to Anton, 'How could you do that? We had a good safe stay there and now we're in the middle of nowhere. It's risky, we could be picked up any time, as soon as we find a suitable place, we have to shoot each other.' We got a lift in an army truck and hopped out between Orol and Bryansk, near the highway. We found a bushy valley a few hundred metres from the road, which seemed ideal for our plan so we slept there. Next morning, the weather had changed. It was stormy and showery with rolls of thunder, and I said to Anton, 'Today is the day, it's just the right weather, nobody will take any notice of rifle shot, with thunder around. Where do you want me to shoot you?'

His face went white. 'I think in my left arm.'

And I told him, 'I want it in my right foot, you have to shoot me first, after I shoot you in the arm, you won't be able to shoot properly.' Anton was a very bad marksman and from only five metres (5½ yards) away, his shot went between my legs. I was pretty strung up and yelled at him, 'What kind of an idiot are you! Try again and do it properly!' This time the bullet went through my foot, below where I wanted it, but I was happy with the result. The rest was simple—I took up my rifle and said, 'Put your arm out.' He turned around with his back to me, shaking with fright. I said 'That's no good, turn around, you have to look at me when I shoot.' I took aim and shot exactly in the spot he chose. He was crying from the strain of the whole thing. I said, 'Anton, I'm leaving first, I'll hail a truck to give me a lift to Briansk, you come up a bit later.'

He wept and said, 'I want us to go together.'

'We can't go together,' I yelled, 'They'd know we shot each other.' I limped up to the main road and the good luck that favoured me so often favoured me again as a Red Cross vehicle delivering wounded soldiers to the next hospital in Briansk stopped for me. I never saw nor heard of Anton again, I hope he got through. I was delivered to a First Aid station where the orderly in charge questioned me. I told him I was wounded at the front by a random enemy shot. I had no papers but he was friendly and accepted everything I told him, I thought maybe with the war going against us that he was disillusioned with the Nazis. He dressed the bullet wound as it had gone through the inside of my left foot and out the other side. As I lay comfortably on the treatment table, I discovered what the friendly orderly really wanted when he began running his hands over me, doing his best to stimulate me. He had no hope! My mind was totally set against him.

The orderly put me, along with hundreds of other soldiers on a train that brought us straight to Austria, to a hospital 50 kilometres (31 miles) from Vienna. We were treated by friendly doctors and nurses and I picked up bits of their conversation, which was all anti-Nazi and anti-war. There was one radio in the ward of about 50 soldiers and I wrangled to get it next to my bed. Friends gathered round and we listened very quietly every night to Radio London. The war news was good, for the first time we heard of victories by the Allies. When Hitler came on Radio Breslau, ranting about Germany's superiority, and shrieking 'the great German race will win the war', voices broke into the radio band, saying mockingly, 'Oh no it won't!' and other cheeky denials of his passionate proclamations. This kind of thing lifted our spirits skywards and made the much longed-for end of the war seem closer.

I was aware of a corporal watching me from his bed on the other side of the ward. With my aptitude in radio technology, I was able to distort Hitler's broadcasts coming into the wards and one night when we had our ears tuned to London, he burst out furiously, 'I know what you are doing and I will bring you where you belong!' Four years later, I chanced to meet him in the market place in Düsseldorf when everything was over. I was selling rollmops and, as he approached, he stopped and looked at me. His eyes said, 'Is this you?' and my eyes said, 'Yes it's me and I don't want to know you.' In later years, I grew more tolerant.

In January 1943, the tide in the east had turned against Hitler. Stalingrad was in the hands of the Red Army. In Africa, where the battle lines had been stretching and contracting like a piano accordion, the British General Montgomery finally had Rommel, the Desert Fox, and our troops in retreat. German planes and ships no longer controlled the sea and air. I was glad—I wanted the Allies to be victorious, I wanted the war over, I wanted Germany to be free of the Nazis. What had they done for my country but let loose a reign of terror on the Jews and every outspoken liberal thinker.

It was wise for anyone with liberal ideas to keep them very much to oneself, but I couldn't help myself. In hospital, I hobbled around the ward, talking to anyone with an interest in politics. I discovered a soldier from Thurau in Saxony named Egon Barr who was an outspoken anti-Fascist. Of the Austrians who were pro-Nazi, Egon observed, 'They lift their arms in the Hitler salute even higher than the Germans!' His family was middle class with a political affinity to the Social Democratic party and after the war Egon became a minister in the German Reichstag.

The walking wounded, or the hobbling wounded in my case, had a treat once a week, having a choice of operas, dramas, films or comic operas. Enjoying Franz Lehar's *Merry Widow* was a big improvement on facing the Russians at the front! My fiancée Annie came and visited me in hospital, still very upset with my mother. I tried to comfort her—I understood Mother but I loved Annie. During this time, soldiers were receiving telegrams from home when there was damage to their houses from allied bombs. The hospital authorities granted the army leave to re-establish some order so I rang Mother and urged her to send me a telegram. Mother, ever helpful, obliged. It came shortly afterwards saying, 'Bruno come home ... you are needed urgently!' I copied the postmistress's handwriting and added, 'Total destruction'.

I took it to the hospital administrator who read it and said, 'O.K., come over at four o'clock, all your papers will be signed and you can have leave for four weeks.' I took the train from Vienna to Nienburg, about 800 kilometres (500 miles). It was beautiful to be home again, Mother and my sister Hilly were there. Mother had sold her shop by now, she was getting too old. Hilly was still working in the Junkers aircraft factory as a technical draftswoman.

I got Mother aside and told her I wasn't going back to the front. Her eyes grew wide with concern as she looked at me, many things

MAJ-R
THRIFT
KANSAS CITY KS

12/29/2015   000000
#2040   3:05PM SERV 01 0001

MISC   1$14.99
NEW 5   1 $5.00
MENS   1 $3.99
                   50.00%
50% DISC   1 2.00
BINS   1 $3.99
MDSE S1 $25.97
TAX1 $2.66

**TOTAL $28.63
CASH $40.00
CHANGE $11.37

must have gone through her mind, but she said nothing so I took her silence as consent.

Not many of my Communist friends were left, they were forced into fighting for the Nazis in Communist Russia. I thought why hadn't they taken the risk and done what I had done? I made the most of my leave from the army and had a great time—eating, drinking, sleeping. I told my friends how I had slipped through the army net and they laughed and I laughed and we drank a lot of beer. Looking back, nobody could say I fought at the front, for the time I was there, I helped to make up the numbers.

DESERTION

After my four weeks leave was over, instead of going back to the army, I went to see my good friend Gunter Lages who was a warden in Sigberg prison camp. I stayed with him a few days and told him that, for me, the war is over. 'Everybody can see it, we've lost Stalingrad, there's light at the end of the tunnel.' Gunter agreed, but he was still in the grip of the army. He advised me to go to his father in Düsseldorf who would be sympathetic and willing to help me find cover from the military police. I was realistic enough to know what sort of life was ahead of me and I thanked Gunter and said I would seek his father out. But first, I had to see my sweetheart, Annie.

In December 1943, she was living with her mother in Calw, a little town in the Black Forest and in the following winter, I joined them there. It was a joyful reunion and Annie and I lived openly like a married couple. Our life together was lovely for several months, we were surrounded by beautiful scenery and took long walks in the forest. We planned to marry after the war when I could justify my desertion.

After a time, Annie's mother, Matilda became a trial, seeming to welcome spats with our neighbours. She quarrelled with two other families living in the same block of flats and also with people in the close neighbourhood. She offended one of them, an elderly man, calling him an *alter esel* (old donkey). He became so incensed that he walked a couple of kilometres to the town to report her to the police. Contact with the police was the last thing I wanted. I had no legal papers and, if caught, I faced a quick execution, no trial, just the death sentence carried out next morning. I resented the turmoil Mathilda was causing and said to Annie, 'Let's go to Switzerland, we'll walk there.'

We hadn't gone far down the road when Annie stopped, her eyes sad. 'What will Mother do? I'm the only one she's got.' So back we went and tried to please her mother but it didn't work. Annie arranged for me to stay with some Yugoslav friends who lived in an old, disused hotel in Horb, 40 kilometres (25 miles) further south. I moved in and found it spacious and comfortable, a real sanctuary. I stayed there for a while and Annie came over every week. Mother sent me money and ration coupons through Hans Scherler, a Communist friend living in Nienburg so my whereabouts could not be traced. But I grew uneasy, it was the beginning of summer in 1944 and the war was still going on. I was a deserter and alert eyes and ears were everywhere, and for reasons of safety, I had to move on. To take Annie with me would be dangerous for us both.

'We'll take up together after the war,' I promised her, but circumstances worked against us. There was the uncertainty of the war and the dangerous situation I was in. I did not write to Annie for fear my letters would come into the possession of the Gestapo and my future with Annie became a dream. My next move was to Düsseldorf.

In June 1944, I caught the express train from Stuttgart to Düsseldorf, a bigger town where detection would be less likely—my friend Gunter's parents lived there. Taking a train was dangerous as they were closely watched and passengers were constantly checked for their papers and movements but I decided to take the risk. I boarded the train and got into a middle carriage, keeping a sharp look out for military police, 'chain dogs' as we called them. Then luck deserted me, my heart pounded as I saw two of them entering my carriage at the far end. I could see one checking every passenger's papers and the other standing at the doorway, blocking it so no one could pass without a check.

I began sweating, all the time they were moving closer and closer to me. I stared hard out the window, desperately hoping to see the next station coming where I could hop out and re-enter the train in the front carriage. But there was no stop, the train sped smoothly and I was trapped. The long stretch of line between Stuttgart and Düsseldorf was selected deliberately by the military police so no one could alight and escape detection. I got up quickly and moved through all the carriages of the train to the last compartment in the last carriage, my heart hammering as the two officers steadily made their way towards me. This was the end for me, I could go no further. I felt like a trapped bird, waiting to be killed.

They were gradually coming closer and soon were in the compartment next to mine. I could see their braided uniforms and badges of authority and I vividly pictured myself arrested, handcuffed and taken off by them. Suddenly, a miracle happened—I felt the train slow down and gradually stop. I saw the police walk out and stand on the platform, watching everyone boarding the train. Hastily I returned to my middle compartment and sat down, breathing fast with relief, unable to believe my good luck, hoping it would hold. Not one of my travelling companions had missed me or knew what ordeal I'd been through. The train stopped at Mainz on the river Rhine, half way to Düsseldorf. I didn't take my eyes off the military police, ready to jump off the moment I saw them approaching me. They seated themselves in one of the comfortable carriages, satisfied they had made a thorough search of the train.

At Düsseldorf, I cautiously left the train, avoiding the ticket barrier as military police were standing there checking everyone going through. Instead I walked to the waiting room and ordered a glass of beer. Another customer was at the bar, a woman who sidled up and sat on the stool next to me. I soon knew why: 'You can have my body,' she cooed, 'I need the money, it won't cost you much.' Sex was the last thing on my mind! To me she looked repulsive after Annie's fresh face and desirable body. I gave the willing lady a bit of money and she left. I planned to catch the next train to Ratingen, about 18 kilometres (11 miles) south of Düsseldorf. By now it was dark, too late for the train to Ratingen so I spent the night on a hard bench in the waiting room.

Next day the world seemed a much safer place. I had no trouble finding Gunter's parents' place in Ratingen and bowled up to their front door dressed in civilian clothes and carrying a walking stick. I had carefully observed the dress of men in ordinary employment and decided to wear nothing or do nothing that would draw attention to myself. Gunter's father Peter opened the door. 'I'm a friend of Gunter's, he was my mate at the Lipstadt hospital,' I explained.

'Well, come in, come in!' Peter's welcome was as warm as his cosy house and when I explained my situation, he was very willing to help me. I told Mary, Peter's wife, a nice quiet woman, all about Mother and my home and she willingly accepted me because of my friendship with her son. Peter was leading a careful life, his Communist beliefs were held in abeyance as he performed his duties as an army sergeant at the local military headquarters. One day he received a letter from Gunter who was now at the Russian Front.

'You wouldn't believe how primitive the Russian peasants live,' he wrote to his father.

Peter was extremely upset, 'He's been injected with the Nazi virus,' he roared, throwing the letter down. I gave him my view that it was too soon to expect Russia to catch up with the modern world. 'Russia's a large country and the government needs more time to modernise, we can't expect them to achieve the culture we've got in middle Europe, it took thousands of years to develop,' I reasoned.

What I said made no difference, Peter held onto his dream and I couldn't blame him for that. His wife Mary was a strict Catholic and their differences on the totally opposing philosophies of Communism and Catholicism had not been settled—both held strongly to their separate faiths. Peter confided, 'Mary doesn't go out much, except to church, that's all ... church, church, church!' Most days during my stay with them, I sat around listening to Radio London.

During my first night in Ratingen, there was a British air raid and bombs fell close to Peter's house. Every night thereafter, British bombers came over and dropped heavy loads of bombs on the town. The noise was awful and people lived in fear of the nights. Peter and I and those living close crammed into his cellar and as the bombs exploded, people screamed in anger at the pilots. I was angry too but my feeling was directed against the Nazis whose whole fanatical idealism had led us into hell's fire. I couldn't help myself, I shouted, 'Why can't they finish the war, these bloody Nazis, why can't they give up!'

Peter grabbed me and hissed in my ear, 'Shut up, stop this stupid talking! I don't know who's a Nazi here and who's not, it's not just your safety you're risking, it's mine and Mary's as well!' I knew he was right, but at times I found it hard to control my feelings. My life was not mine to control and all I could do was try to hide from the war going on around me.

It was summer and for three peaceful weeks while staying with Peter, we enjoyed good weather. Suddenly Germany rocked apart with the news of a plot to assassinate Hitler. A bomb planted close to him had unfortunately missed its target. 'The devil looks after his own,' Peter muttered. As details of the plotters emerged, we learned the aristocratic Claus Schenk Graf von Stauffenberg and other highly respected German army officers were involved, having decided to rid Germany of Hitler's terrible influence. This was opposition at the highest level, and it suggested that Hitler was not as unassailable as he appeared to be. The might of the Nazi regime was still intact and I was not out of its grip yet.

One day Peter said, 'The neighbours will become suspicious of you, we'll have to find other places for you to stay. Don't worry, I have plenty of friends in Düsseldorf.' He introduced me to his Communist friends and they generously offered me accommodation at great risk to their lives. I moved from one place to another on a weekly basis and this fine lot of people harboured me safely for the best part of two years. One of them, Hans Baur, gave me the key to his flat on the ground floor of a three-storey house. He was a cabinetmaker, a middle-aged tradesman who made beautiful furniture. We talked for hours on politics. I said to him, 'Everywhere I go, I find friendly people who are against the war.'

'Yes,' he said sagely, 'They can see the wool floating away.' This was an old German saying, which meant in this case, the tide had turned against Nazism. He added with a cynical smile, 'At times, one must howl with the wolves.'

During this time, although it wasn't wise, I wrote letters to friends in Nienburg. Communicating by post was very risky but I wanted them to understand it was my hatred of the Nazis' total military power that motivated my desertion. I addressed one to Herr Scharf, our butcher. His son, Wilhelm, was a schoolmate of mine, but in the post-war years, gave me the cold shoulder because I had deserted. Mother told me later how she had entered Herr Scharf's crowded butcher shop and his wife had said in a pleased voice, 'Mrs Trappmann, we've got a letter from your son.' Mother said there was total silence and all the customers turned their eyes on her, the mother of the son who had deserted the army. They must have been a decent lot because no one informed the Gestapo about it.

While I was in hiding, I had plenty of time to think. I missed my freedom of movement but was very willing to put up with it to be out of the battle zones. Of course my absence at the front was recorded and the 'chain dogs' tried to hunt me down. After the war when I returned home, I was told the Nazi who worked at the gas factory in Nienburg had been contacted by the military police. He turned up on Mother's doorstep, asking my whereabouts and Mother, with much presence of mind, professed ignorance and said to him, 'If you find out where my son is, please let me know.'

All this time I was acting the part of a wounded soldier, always walking with a stick. Before I left one place, to account for my regular absences, I told the tenants I had to go back to the hospital for treatment. Things were going well for me, Mother was still sending me money and I had no further close shaves with the military police to make me uneasy. Then I heard over the radio that 4,000 ships had landed on the coast of Normandy.

At last! Great news! Anti-Nazis could celebrate everywhere. Soon I could go back to my lovely hometown, Nienburg. I could feel freedom flowing towards me, but war was not over just yet. My identity as a wounded soldier could not be abandoned, there were still a lot of Nazis, still a lot of believers. They pinned their hopes on the V-1 rocket, a pilotless plane like a flying bomb, which had just been launched against London. Those rockets caused a lot of damage but nothing could stop the Allied advance.

Suddenly, in the last months of Nazi power, when its massive power structure was tottering under attack from Allies in the west and Russians in the east, my life once again hung by a thread. At the time I was living in my friend Paul's flat in Flingern, a suburb of Düsseldorf. He was unfit for military service and lived and worked in the countryside with his wife and child and came over to Flingern for a couple of days every so often.

Paul and I, on that memorable day, chose a nice pub in Düsseldorf to relax over a few beers. We settled down comfortably at a table facing the entrance. I felt a close trust existing between us, an understanding between two people who shared the same ideals. Paul twirled his beer and looked at me closely and from his demeanour I knew he had something on his mind.

'You know Bruno, I wonder about this life you're leading.' He grinned wryly, 'All this ducking around, giving the Gestapo the slip, is it worth it? You know they usually catch deserters.'

I shook my head vigorously. 'I have to do it, Paul.'

'I know you do.' He bent towards me and lowered his voice. 'What you are doing will cut you off from everyone,' he said regretfully. 'You have deserted your mates as well as the Nazi army and you will be judged harshly for that, condemned as a coward.'

Without hesitation, I defended myself. 'Listen Paul, I only have one life and I made a choice what to do with it. I don't want to fight in any war and there's no way I could fight in this war. It's all wrong!'

My breath was coming fast, I could feel my face burning with outrage. 'What are our troops doing in Russia, what have the poor illiterate Russian peasants done to us? Stalin hasn't taken any German territory, Hitler's the aggressor, hell-bent on grabbing Russian land and crushing communism,' I hissed. Waves of anger scorched through me at the thought of being a puppet to serve Nazi ideals. I felt like shouting my objections in the tightly packed room.

Paul nodded in understanding and grabbed my glass to refill it. Suddenly he stiffened, his eyes widened and I immediately sensed danger. Following his gaze I saw three military police standing at the entrance, one officer and two soldiers. My heart began to race as they started a thorough check of everyone in the bar room. The officer and a soldier went from table to table, leaving one soldier standing at the door so no one could leave without having their papers checked.

I whispered to Paul, 'I have to get out! I'll try the back way.' I went into the toilet and saw the window was barred. No chance. I rushed to the back entrance but the door was locked and barred. I was in a dilemma, I rejoined Paul, feeling desperate, 'Ach ach, there's no way out, I'm gone, soon they'll be here at our table!' All at once I saw a group of people coming in through the front door and the soldier there was busy looking through their papers. 'This is my only chance,' I hissed to Paul, getting up. With as much calm as I could muster, I walked slowly passed the guard as though I had nothing to hide, like a bonafide wounded soldier. As soon as I was out into the street and round the corner, I put my walking stick under my arm and ran. How I ran! I haven't run like it since. I hopped onto the next tram and arrived home at Paul's place. I got into bed and stilled my racing heart, then a feeling of euphoria swept over me, I had slipped through the Nazi net again. I was still savouring my escape when Paul came home after midnight

Desertion

He couldn't stop laughing, 'Bruno, I thought that was the end of you.' He opened a bottle, shook his head and looked at me with a serious light in his eyes. 'I don't know how you're going to make it through,' he clinked his glass against mine, 'but good luck. Here's to you beating the *Arschlöcher* (arseholes)!' I downed the toast with great gusto.

Before I went to sleep, I thought of Annie. In my moments of solitude, I longed for a female companion. I had good mates but there was nothing like the love of a girl to make life complete. Next day, I left Paul's flat and returned to Peter and Mary's. I boarded a tram and saw the loveliest girl in the world and straight away I was smitten! The tram conductress uniform she was wearing could not disguise her lissome body and grace of movement. My heart missed a beat as she gazed at me with heavenly blue eyes so all day long I travelled on that tram to the terminus and back, striking up conversation, trying to break down her reserve. Next day, I was on the tram again, persuading her to meet me after work and finally she agreed. But alas, she didn't turn up.

I said to Peter, 'I am miserable. I am in love with a girl but she won't see me.'

He was very angry and glared at me. 'What do you think you're doing? You can't afford to have love affairs—this girl could put you in danger. You want to live don't you? You have to stay out of it. The war will be over soon and you want to be alive to see it.' I could see the sense of Peter's words, but words couldn't control the emotions flowing from my heart. At such times, a normal life seemed illusory and I vowed to myself, when again I possessed the things I most cherished, I would value them and never let them go.

I moved about, taking many precautions not to reveal myself as a deserter, but my life was lived on a knife's edge. Anyone could suddenly realise who I was and inform on me. It was my custom to go to Frau Becker's flat on the top floor of a large house for lunch, but this day she appeared at the top of the stairs, waving me away.

'Bruno, don't come here, the local policeman told me to tell you to go back to Flingern. He said if you came he would have to arrest you.' She caught my arm, breathless and very agitated. 'Someone from this house put you in, it's sure to be that Nazi from Aachen.'

'Who is he? How does he know about me?'

'The brewery driver's wife lives downstairs, it's her brother, he's a *Kreisleiter* (the chief district officer of the Nazi party in Aachen).' She looked quickly around. 'I'd hate you to be caught, just go … go!' Hurriedly I thanked her and left, my arrest would mean a swift and fatal vengeance for my months of freedom.

I went back to Paul's place in Flingern and kept out of sight for a few days. News came over the radio that the Russians were sweeping towards Berlin. Great! But where were the Western allies? They should be approaching to occupy German territory from the west, the Russians were doing all the right things, what were the Allies waiting for? At last the good news came. The Allied forces had crossed the Rhine. Most bridges over the Rhine had been blown up by the German army, but by default a bridge at Remagen had been left intact and it was here the Allies poured over and were making rapid progress into Germany.

CLOSER TO VICTORY

Early in 1945, the Americans occupied France. I was elated to learn the Americans were only two or three kilometres west of Düsseldorf. They bombarded us day and night with artillery fire and a few times grenades exploded in the street close to Peter's house. One day I took a bit of a walk through a shopping centre and suddenly motorbikes and sidecars with machine guns mounted roared down the road. American soldiers waved people aside. 'Clear off, get inside or we'll shoot you!' I took cover and peered out at them, they were looking for signs of armed resistance and I waited to see what they would do. After an hour or two, with no opposition, they formed up and marched through the middle of the town. People ventured out and lined the streets, waving and welcoming them.

Three days later, they occupied all of Düsseldorf and the town was liberated! I threw my walking stick in the air and people stared and said, 'Oh, you can walk! It's a miracle!' 'Yes,' I said, 'Liberation does miraculous things. The war is over.'

Events happened quickly after that. I went back to Ratingen and traded my radio for a bicycle. Before leaving Düsseldorf, I said goodbye to Peter, Mary, Paul and Hans and thanked them all. Then I went to visit the friendly policeman who had warned me to stay away from Frau Becker's place. He was now in American custody at Kaiserswerth, 30 kilometres (19 miles) from Düsseldorf. He had saved my life and I thought I could put a good word in for him. He came out and spoke to me, saying he did not want his timely warning to be a topic of conversation.

'The war is still on, Bruno, keep your head down, we've got Nazis among us here and in Düsseldorf. Be careful, they could still harm you.' In hindsight, I think he realised the help he had given me could make him a target for revengeful Nazis. I thanked the friendly policeman once more and wished him good fortune.

Soon after, extensive prisoner-of-war camps were established and run by the British in north Germany, but German army officers were not disarmed. Consequently, some of the most fanatical Nazis passed sentence on those they considered had sinned against the Fatherland (such as deserters) and shot them.

I was in a highly excited state of mind as I thought of returning home, it was 12 April 12 1945, my sister Hilly's birthday. I heard over the radio that the Americans had entered Nienburg and I knew she would be celebrating their arrival. I hopped on my bicycle and cycled towards home with a light heart, singing as I rode, knowing Mother was waiting to welcome me. It took me four days to cover the distance of 500 kilometres (310 miles). I slept in the open and several times obliging farmers let me sleep on the hay in their sheds. Not far out of Düsseldorf, some British soldiers stopped me at a checkpoint and wanted to see my papers. I explained I was a deserter from the army, but they arrested me and I was taken into the official building and put in a room by myself. The British officials didn't know what to do with me and were waiting for their officer in charge to turn up. I was impatient at this delay, filled with an urgent desire to reach home. I could see no one was checking on me, security was lax so I quietly walked out, jumped on my bicycle and was off home, taking a back road through the forest.

As I rode, I could just glimpse the main road with the British patrol driving up and down searching for me. I laughed at my escape and peddled steadily towards Nienburg, now only 300 kilometres (186 miles) away. I met no more obstacles and in a few days I reached home. Mother was overjoyed to see me, and Hilly and I talked all night, we had so much to tell each other. I learned Nienburg was in American hands, the Nazis formerly in control had hastily cleared off to the West and our bürgermeister, Herr Schulz, had done likewise.

My first visit was to my good old loyal Communist friend, Hans Scherler, who without fail, all the time I was in hiding, had picked up money from my mother and sent it to me. I met a dozen of my old comrades, who had hidden their Communist links and led a very careful life under Nazi rule. A few of them were grabbed by the army and ended up as prisoners-of-war in a Russian camp. I was something of a hero having survived the Nazi regime with a death sentence over my head. I was so grateful to the comrades who had sheltered me regardless of the great personal risk they took and I would always feel indebted to them.

The war was coming to an end now, with most of Germany in the Allies' hands. The Red Army was closing in on Berlin and Hitler had only a few days to live. I looked around the familiar streets of my hometown and saw there was not much war damage. One bomb dropped by the RAF had completely destroyed the hotel on the outskirts of town; another landed in the middle of the main street, killing one of our policemen who had been on duty going from pub to pub, checking on their closing times. Mother's shop window was blown in with the percussion from the explosion and a third bomb destroyed some houses.

As I wandered around, I wondered what had happened to Annie. There was no normal flow of mail between east and west Germany where I had left her. During the time of our separation, I had been too pre-occupied with my own safety to think much about her. I now faced the fact that I no longer cared; our romance was over, killed by our separation.

As luck would have it, a letter arrived from one of our neighbours in the Black Forest where we had stayed, giving me news. Annie was getting married to a French soldier from Morocco and was going back to live with him there. I was relieved to hear it and wrote back, congratulating her and wishing her happiness in her marriage and new life.

Not long after, another letter arrived from Peter Lages giving me the sad news that my good friend Hans Bauer had died, but also some quite inspirational details of Hans' activities. Before he died, he had organised a big Freedom March in Düsseldorf for everyone to participate and celebrate the victory over Nazism. Peter had enclosed a long newspaper article and a photo of Hans carrying a painting of Heinrich Heine, the well-known Jewish writer born in Düsseldorf. It was great to know that Hans, a well-respected Communist with years of political struggle behind him, had right up until his death, been true to his ideals. He was a real inspiration to me and I hoped I could be as good a man, living up to his standards.

I had been home for about four weeks when I had a love affair with a girl named Ursula I met at my neighbour Heinz' party. She was a nurse from Bernburg, very attractive and very well educated. I took her home, knowing Mother would think, at last Bruno has chosen the right type of girl for himself. I felt very satisfied with life, I was young, I had my health and Hitler's regime, his grand design for the Third Reich to conquer the world had collapsed in total and humiliating defeat. Now I had captured Ursula, this lovely girl with a combination of beauty and brains. She set my heart singing with her charming vivaciousness and gaiety and in just four weeks, I'd asked her to marry me.

One Saturday afternoon we went to the Four Corners inn, which was packed with locals and a handful of American soldiers. With the sound of music and the harmonious buzz of people's voices we enjoyed our drinks and the company of friends. Looking into Ursula's dark eyes, I saw my happy future there and thought how lucky I was. She had a restless beauty, her eyes flashed around the room, her lips curved in a brilliant welcoming smile and I felt proud that she attracted admiring glances. We got pleasantly tipsy and time flew by unnoticed.

When Ursula rose to go to the bathroom, I also excused myself. The male and female bathrooms were separated by a wall and, as I relieved myself, I heard voices in the ladies bathroom. I recognised Ursula's voice and then with a prickling sensation, I realised a man was in there with her. I held my breath and listened incredulously. I couldn't believe what I was hearing, the man's voice, low and coaxing, my fiancée laughing softly, teasing him. I trembled with shock as I heard her suggest they postpone intimacy until the following day. I knew she was with a Yankee soldier and I was outraged. How could this be? I went quickly to our table, said goodbye to my friends and stamped out of the pub, full of rage. Before I went far, I heard running footsteps behind me.

Ursula caught my arm. 'What's happened, where are you going?' I swung round and when she saw my face, she knew. She was an intelligent woman, what could she say? I never saw her again. About a year later, I heard she died of pneumonia.

BRUNHILDE

Sometime later, I was having a beer in the Spring Hotel, and became interested in a couple of girls sitting at a table near the window. I particularly liked the look of one of them with dark hair curling around her smooth face. Her eyes seemed to invite me so I took my beer and went over. I guess at that moment more than anything I wanted to forget the war and forget what Hitler had done to our country. Soon we were talking and laughing and as I looked into the brilliant eyes of the attractive, dark-haired girl, it struck me that the thing I wanted most was a good home life with a loving wife.

Next day the girls were again there and we took walks together. Brunhilde, the dark-haired one I sized up as a good, working-class girl and after two weeks I asked her to marry me. She took me home to meet her mother, Bernadine, a little fat talkative lady, the mother of nine children, five sons and four daughters. Brunhilde was the second last girl. The family had moved from the Ruhr Valley because of continuous bombing by the British Air Force. They were sick of alarm bells and sitting long hours in cellars. Because Nienburg offered Brunhilde's father, a miner, no alternative employment, he remained there working in the Valley mines.

One day when I visited the family, Bernadine created a scene. She looked grimly at Brunhilde and said, 'I haven't seen your bloodstained linen this month, where is it?' Brunhilde mumbled something, and her mother said loudly, 'I hope you're not pregnant, have you had your monthlies?'

Brunhilde shook her head.

'There! You are pregnant!' Bernadine turned a red angry face on me and I sensed the scene was a bit of an act for my benefit. Next day Bernadine went to the Nienburg Council. 'My daughter's three months pregnant,' she declared, demanding extra food coupons. Hilly was working in the Council at this time, giving out ration coupons, and heard about Bernadine's visit. She bailed me up that evening.

'What's this about Brunhilde being three months pregnant? Do you really think it's your child?'

'Yes I do.'

Hilly looked sceptical. 'You haven't known her for three months, just work it out.'

Doubt was beginning to cloud my mind. Brunhilde was beginning to show and Nienburg was humming with gossip. My friend Hans Schlerer said to me, 'She's been playing up and she's grabbed you to get her out of the mess!' Then Mother started on me. 'It's a pity you picked up this little working-class girl when you could have had someone like Ursula. She had character!'

I felt my face flushing with rage. 'Oh yes,' I retorted, 'A bad one!' I was still smarting over what that young woman had done to me. I think Mother welcomed the mess I was in and hoped it would bring an end to my affair with Brunhilde.

'Don't see Brunhilde,' she advised, 'Stay away from her, it won't be your child.'

I was sick of all this and I asked Brunhilde directly, 'Tell me, is it my child?'

'Of course it is!' Her eyes darkened, she was very upset. 'I haven't been with anyone else, what do you take me for!' I should have believed her, but poisonous doubts worked on my mind. I remembered how I was fooled over Charlotte and Ursula. I wasn't going to be humiliated for a third time.

I went to see Bernadine and told her I couldn't be the father of Brunhilde's child. 'She's too far gone, it can't be mine. I'm breaking off our engagement.'

Bernadine glared at me as though I was the biggest fool. 'My daughter's not three months pregnant,' she said. 'I went to the Council and pitched them a tale to get extra food coupons.' She flung the door open and said 'Just wait, you'll see! Time will tell who the father is!' I didn't see Bernadine for years after that, as the family returned to the Ruhr Valley. Brunhilde moved in with her elder sister Irmguarde and they stayed in Nienburg.

I threw myself full-time into trading black market goods in Berlin. I didn't visit Brunhilde; instead I drank with my friends at night and tried to forget her. Then one day Irmguarde went to see Mother and poured out her heart. 'Your son has made my sister pregnant, she's seven months gone now and he's not even interested to see her. She feels completely deserted, she weeps every day and can't understand why Bruno has abandoned her.'

Mother was convinced by Irmguarde's sincerity and said to me, 'You have to marry Brunhilde, it must be your child.' Then she gave me her blessing and began to make ready a flat in her house for us.

Brunhilde

Mother's plea had convinced me to go to Brunhilde. I might never know if the child was mine, but I couldn't forget her as easily as I had wanted. We had a big party the night before the wedding, Mother and my sisters, my partner Hans and all my friends came and we had a great time. Food and drinks, possible through my black market trading, were laid on and we drank and sang till the early hours. Next morning, feeling weak and sober, I dressed for my wedding. The ceremony was arranged for 10 a.m. in the Council reception rooms by Nienburg's bürgermeister. My car stopped on the way. It ran on charcoal and I had to jump out and stoke up the burner. When I arrived, Brunhilde laughed, 'Look at you, covered in soot, what a bridegroom!' Hilly and her current boyfriend were our witnesses.

After the ceremony, all four of us piled into my car and we drove to the Harz Mountains, 50 kilometres (31 miles) away. There we discovered every hotel was booked out, the only accommodation offering was one room in a guesthouse with two beds. After hours of celebrating with as much style as the hotel's fare would allow, we headed back to the poor accommodation and fell exhausted into our beds.

Next morning after breakfast, all of us went for a walk in beautiful sunshine. We reached a grassy glen and Hilde, who had participated in many nudist camps, without hesitation stripped off her clothes, whereupon Ernst, her boyfriend, followed suit, but not Brunhilde. I suggested we enjoy the sun on our bodies, but she strongly objected. Nudity, she believed was an immoral oddity the rich indulged in, running about without their clothes and exhibiting all sorts of dubious behaviour.

Time passed by quickly and happily with my new bride, her youthful body pulsing and growing large with our baby. One night, several months later, Brunhilde shook me awake. 'It's coming, it's coming,' she gasped. One contraction following quickly upon another and I hastened to Frau Veckenstedt, the midwife a few streets away.

'Have you got hot water ready?' she asked me sharply as we returned to Mother's house. I had trouble keeping up with her, a tall heavily built woman who delivered, on average, three babies per week in Nienburg.

I shook my head, confessing I hadn't the slightest idea of what I should do to assist Brunhilde.

'It's not for her, I want a good cup of coffee. See to it!' she said irritably. As soon as she strode to Brunhilde's side she became instantly professional, examining Brunhilde and asssuring me everything was satisfactory. Mother's flat was next to ours and I wondered if I should wake her and let her know her grandchild was on the way.

But I didn't need to, Brunhilde's screams soon woke Mother up but she stayed in her bed and I left everything to Frau Veckenstedt. She told Brunhilde to grip the wooden bed rail as each contraction came. Poor Brunhilde, she was having a torturous time, panting and sweating, her hair sticking to her wet forehead, screaming with the pain of each strong contraction. I was appalled by what she was going through, all I could do was hold her hand.

'Take a deep breath and push Mrs Trappmann, you're nearly there,' urged Frau Veckenstedt. Brunhilde gave a final loud scream and our child emerged into the world. I goggled at my baby daughter, so tiny, so inhuman, so like a rabbit!

Brunhilde was laughing excitedly exclaiming, 'A girl ... a girl ... a girl!' Frau Veckenstedt bustled around, fixing the baby, attending to Brunhilde. She thrust the afterbirth at me.

'Throw it into the river, it will bring you good luck!' I went over the bridge next to the flour mill and aimed it far into the water. It landed on a rock protruding from the middle of the river. I waited to see if the strong current flowing swiftly past would dislodge it, but no, the residue of Brunhilde's labour stuck fast to the top of the rock for every passer-by to see. It sat there for a couple of days as the river birds pecked and pulled at it, then the scrappy remains sank to the bottom for the fish to devour.

I felt proud of becoming a father and looked my little girl over carefully. She was perfectly made. Then I saw something that, had I still been in doubt about her parentage, would have proved it beyond any doubt. On both the baby's feet, two of her tiny toes were joined for a fraction of the way. My toes are the same, as are my mother's toes. It is a family gene working through the Trappmann generations.

RUSSIAN OCCUPATION

In the summer of 1945, Germany lay in ruins. Dire misery prevailed. Bombs and artillery shells had reduced the major cities to grotesque heaps of rubble. Apartments and shops, office buildings and factories lay in shambles, water and gas mains were ruptured, electric and telephone wires were cut in thousands of places.

Immediately after the war, a feeling of unrest pervaded our little town. One felt anything could happen and in that uncertain atmosphere, morality broke down. The American soldiers were housed in a substantial school building and girls hung around there to cadge cigarettes, coffee and other luxuries from them. And it wasn't just the girls, married men seemed to be affected by the presence of an occupying army. Facing the uncertainties of Russian occupation, they sought diversionary pleasures with young girls. After three months of U.S. command, the Americans announced they were withdrawing from East Germany and the Russian occupation forces would take over.

They left Nienburg on 1 July 1945 with many tearful German girls waving them goodbye.

For those who were Communists, the imminent arrival of the Russians was welcome news but for many people in Nienburg it produced an element of fear. They took out their Nazi flags and unstitched the Nazi swastika, converting it to an inoffensive red to wave at the Russians from their windows. Looking closely, one could see the shape of the swastika but it didn't create any troublesome events during Russia's occupation.

The day after the U.S. troops left, in came the Russians without any sign of an official party to acknowledge their arrival. Council officials and Nienburg's bürgermeister, appointed by the Americans to replace the Nazi councillors, did not stir from their Council chambers.

The old Communists and I got together and, bearing signs of welcome, met the Russians on the outskirts of Nienburg. Heinrich, Hans, Ernst, Walter, Heinz and many other Lefties, including my sister Hilde, all waited excitedly for the Russians to enter. We hoped sometime in the future our unswerving loyalty to Communist ideologies would bear fruit, like being given positions of authority in the Nienburg council. That's what we thought would occur, but the reality was quite different.

The Russian company and its officers straggled in, out of line, walking loosely with no semblance of military training. One of the soldiers stopped and asked Hans for a cigarette. Their light-coloured uniforms were crumpled and dirty. Their disorderly appearance did not dampen our enthusiasm. This was a great moment—to see them about to take control of our part of Germany. Wilhelm Pieck and Walter Ulbricht, Communist party leaders who had sought refuge in Moscow would soon return to East Berlin to create the new East German government.

I, along with my fellow Communists, sought interviews with the new Russian administration to proudly declare our allegiance to them. They were not impressed with us, after all what proof did we have? I guess they thought anyone could fabricate a story with personal advancement in mind. The new Russian Commandant went ahead and worked out the running of our town with the Council officials already there. We were ignored. An old Social Democrat was appointed as bürgermeister, a man with no interest in politics, a political nothing. His main concern was to rebuild Nienburg, repairing war damage to the town's superstructure, roads and buildings. It was clear that my belief in Communism was not going to give me employment in a local government body. I would have to look further afield to earn my living.

Only two of the Communists scored a Council job—Heinrich Ruder in the Registration Office and my sister Hilde in charge of ration coupons for food and clothing. She was very strict issuing food coupons, but later I saw her dealing leniently with farmers who had supplies of meat and fat and butter. Even an honest person like my sister couldn't resist a bit of black-market food.

Corruption of this kind was a common thing all over Germany while food shortages remained. The Russians entrusted keeping the peace in our little town to my friend Karl, whom they appointed as a police sergeant while Ernst and Franz became police constables. Other Party members were sadly disappointed at not being called upon to build our new political regime. The rest of us had to face our disappointments and look further afield to earn our living.

In April 1946, the Russian administration appointed a Coalition Control Board, representing Communists and Social Democrats, under the name of Einheits (Unity Labour Party). A big public meeting was called to merge the Social Democrats with the Communist members. Otto Schulze got up and addressed the public meeting, saying, 'We ex-Nazis want to come back into normal life. You can judge me and decide if I am worthy of public trust.' I was moved by what he said because I knew that despite being a Nazi member, his heart was never in it. On the other hand, his son-in-law, an officer in the Nazi army was a Nazi through and through and later became a councillor for the whole Bernburg district. At our last Party meeting, we sang 'The Internationale' with great gusto and next day joined the Social Democrat party but with far less verve. We thought things might change for the better, but many post-war problems faced the government bodies.

When I had returned to Nienburg after my two-year desertion, I renewed my friendship with Heinz Kuhle, a Communist sympathiser who worked as a clerk at the Court House in Bernburg. Heinz' father-in-law, Heinrich Reinhard was a top Nazi, who made himself scarce before the Russians arrived.

One man not corrupted under Nazi rule was Judge Stutt of Bernburg, whom I had met at Heinz Kuhle's place with other friends about a week after the end of the war. I respected the man, impressed by his sense of justice. He had not been a Judge while the country was under Nazi rule and had instead practised law. Explaining his philosophy on the legal system, he said, 'Better let 10 guilty men go than gaol one innocent man.' At that time, all the guilty men, the ex-Nazis, had left us; they were not waiting for punishment at the hands of any judge, Russian or otherwise.

The official interpreter for the Russian officers was well known to the whole town, a young Polish man known by the name of 'Ash Walter'. Each morning he shovelled the residue ash from domestic coal fires stored in large brick containers at the back of each Nienburg dwelling. I never saw him without a fine light covering of ash on his coat, hair and eyebrows, even when he dressed up, he seemed to me to have a distinctly 'ashy' appearance!

Under Russian occupation we had little choice in food and longed for some variety. Hans Scherle worked in the malt factory, which was used for food storage, and knew the workings of the place inside-out. Our dull diet got the better of a group of us and we decided with Hans' help to raid the food store. After dark one night, four of us rowed a little boat along the Bode River, past the historical monument, keeping to the deep shadow of the Lutheran church and other buildings lining the bank. A night curfew had been imposed so we were vigilant.

We could see Russian soldiers patrolling the front of the storehouse so slipped round the back where Hans was waiting. 'Take off your boots', he said and led the way upstairs to the third floor. What an impressive sight! Tinned meat was stacked on shelves right to the ceiling. Quickly filling boxes, alert for the sound of a heavy Russian tread, we got out with our prized booty, making our way down the stairs and melting away back into the dark. We rowed back to my car parked out of sight in a dark spot, four of us crammed in, nursing our precious stolen goods. A bottle of schnapps did the rounds and soon we weren't that bothered about the cramped conditions; in fact we spent a merry few hours. I didn't expect we would be badly treated if caught—the Russian soldiers seemed harmless enough. Some rumours of rape circulated in the first weeks of them entering Berlin but I can honestly say I never saw evidence of this criminal behaviour in our town.

Naturally there was fraternisation between Russian officers and some German women, it didn't matter whether the women had Communist or Nazi sympathies, politics wasn't an issue. Post-war, nobody knew what would happen next and casual liaisons were common. You could hear comments like, 'Look at that Nazi woman, she's got a Russian officer now and her poor husband is in prison!' It was a topsy-turvy world.

There were Russian checkpoints every 10 kilometres (6 miles) and at the entrance of every village and town. Soldiers searched each vehicle passing through—a bottle of schnapps was the best thing to have, especially if you were carrying anything illegal. Russian soldiers always wanted something, usually cigarettes or alcohol. If you pulled out a bottle they let you through without searching the car.

One day, my friend Hans proposed that we go to a little town 40 kilometres (25 miles) from Nienburg to buy a wether from a farmer he knew. He, Brunhilde and I got in my car and off we went, soon coming to the first Russian control point. A young Russian soldier came over and checked our papers, making it very obvious he fancied Brunhilde. When he handed our papers back, he squeezed in the car beside her, amorously stroking her cheeks.

'Do something, Bruno!', she hissed at me.

I said to Hans, 'Quick, get out the bottle of schnapps.'

The soldier grabbed it and began gulping it down, draining the lot. He let the bottle fall, completely drunk and fell sound asleep. Brunhilde jumped out, laughing at his sprawling figure and gaping mouth. His soldier mates dragged him out at the next checkpoint, not the least concerned. It was funny to see them trying to decipher my car licence holding it upside down, most of them couldn't read German.

In Nienburg, our social structure began to change dramatically; under Russian influence, the Coalition Control Board announced that private ownership was being phased out. Under the new East German government, Mother's tenants no longer paid her, instead put their rent into the Volksbank. Property owners like Mother only got the equivalent of a pension; her house, shops and garden now belonged to the Control Board. She had to accept it, but not all proprietors were able to live with the changes. When the Nienburg newspaper, owned by Frau Weber's family for generations was taken over, she jumped out of a top-storey window. Shop owners and Nienburg's small inn proprietors, well known for their ability to satisfy customers with a nice meal, beer and schnapps, were forced to go on the black market. I was becoming disenchanted with what was happening in Nienburg under Russian influence.

My dearest wish was that East Germany would emerge as a shining example to the other zones occupied by the British, French and Americans. I imagined that with industry and social services nationalised, all aspects of commerce would pick up and run ahead. Then my countrymen from West Germany would come flooding over and look at our achievements with envious eyes. Unfortunately that was not the case and East Germany was being stripped of many of its assets.

In the West, with the help of American dollars, the economy was picking up, with export and import trade recovering. Money was available to repair war damage. In the East, for reparations, the Russian troops demolished our factories and transported them to Russia. The big OMZ complex, our cement factories, our malt factory and our grain mill all went east. In Bernburg, our nearest town, the Solway factories were dismantled and sent to Russia, even our railway lines were ripped up and taken.

I hoped our former thriving river trade would be restored to full capacity with the destroyed bridges rebuilt but, of the former 202 boat owners, only 93 of them still had their boats. My great-uncle who had plied his boat, the *Gustav Klaus* up and down the Saale River for many years would have been most upset had he lived to see it.

I was pleased when Bertolt Brecht, the famous playwright and his actress wife, Helene Weigel came back to live in East Germany but not at all pleased by the appointment of a former Nazi army General, Bernard Bechler, to the highest rank in the East German army. I guess I just had to accept what was happening around me at this stage of my country's history.

CIVILIAN LIFE

When Herr Schulz, our bürgermeister, left for the West along with other Nazi sympathisers, the local police sergeant filled his place. The sergeant was a likeable person, although in his position of power you couldn't be absolutely sure of him. I wanted to build up a business with my friend Hans Scherler and for this we needed the sergeant's consent. When Mother, always generous to me with money, gave me enough to buy a truck, Hans and I went along to see a man named Walter Pieck in charge of ex-army motor vehicles. There were no trucks or cars for sale, not even spare parts, not even a battery. Food was in short supply and rationing was strictly enforced. The inflationary prices for food items were ridiculous—coffee on the black market was 500 dollars per kilo, a bottle of schnapps 200 dollars, butter 200 dollars per kilo, sugar 60 dollars per kilo and cigarettes, 10 dollars each.

My partner Hans was enterprising. He had been a foreman in an immense food store during the war and somehow managed to get supplies of coffee. We thought it would better our chances of getting a truck if Walter was given this prized item.

His reaction surprised us. 'What do you take me for!' he shouted, his face flushing red. 'I'm not a corrupt person!' His hand shot out and grabbed the coffee.

Next day we got our truck. No petrol was available so we converted the truck to run on timber gas. We obtained a briquette licence from the police sergeant and delivered briquettes to people who were near freezing because of fuel shortages. Coal was in short supply, a lot of it going towards reparations to the Allies. The nearest coal mine was in Nitterfeld where we picked up our first load. When we returned for a second load, the manager told us supply had run out until the following month. We were exasperated, gone were our chances of making a living from coal delivery. Next we tried out the job of furniture removalists but that fizzled out also.

Food rationing under Russian occupation became even more severe and as news filtered through of the better living conditions in the Western part of Germany, a lot of people were interested. I could see the reason for them leaving, many had relations in West Germany and borders created problems for separated families. For Hans and I, this represented a new business opportunity and although transporting people to the border was making money for us, I was opposed to the existence of any border patrolled by police between East and West Allied zones. Like most Germans, I felt this keenly. Never before had we had such irksome restrictions to our travel.

I felt disillusioned with the Russians for creating this barrier, it was the first big thing they did wrong in my eyes. Communists coming from the West were arrested, locked up and next day sent back. By contrast, all of us from East Germany were welcome in the West and I never heard of anyone being sent home. The Russian clampdown on freedom of movement worried me. Freedom on a personal and political level was a precious thing, one of the main issues for any class of people.

Ready to have a go.

We kept our transportation of people very quiet and the authorities did not challenge us, but after a while the stream of people who had relations and other connections in the West lessened and we were again out of work.

Because of the rationing, food was a number one priority. One day, Eddie Tormann, a wholesale vegetable merchant who had good connections with farmers growing onions and potatoes got in touch with us. We bought the produce and sold it to the licensee of a pub in Berlin. This man took it all and sold it on the black market, making 100 per cent profit—it was a booming sellers' market.

Hans and I made regular trips to the American zone of Berlin every fortnight to deliver onions and schnapps. I bought the schnapps from Walter Pieck for 150 dollars a litre. This trade paid well until we got the upsetting news that Walter and his de facto partner had committed suicide. I never found out why they did such a devastating thing.

On the last trip we made selling schnapps to a hotel licensee in Berlin, I had Otto Schult our casual helper with me, which proved lucky. Hans had stacked bags of beech wood all over the car and a bag next to the wood burner caught alight. We pulled over, put the fire out and continued on but it was a slow trip. A bag of wood only took us 20 kilometres before we had to stoke up again. A leaky radiator added to our problems. When we finally arrived, the pub licensee was overjoyed to see us and bought everything we had.

Our car troubles were not over. After we had relaxed for a short while at the pub, the car conked out on the way to our accommodation. I did not like the idea of leaving it on the side of the road in the middle of Berlin but we had no alternative, so we walked to our digs. The next morning I had the feeling we had overslept and roused Otto.

He shrugged me off. 'Can't you see it's dark outside, go back to sleep.'

My gut feeling persisted. During the war, because of the air raids, people stuck black material over their windows, or painted them black. When I got up and flung the door open, strong sunlight flooded in.

'What time is it?' I asked some people passing our room.

'11 o'clock.'

'It's midnight in our room,' I muttered grumpily. I got Otto up and we set off to pick up the car. Along the way, we passed a police station and I was astonished to see our truck parked in the police yard. We didn't fancy being stranded in Berlin so we decided to sneak round the back of the building and make off with it without being seen. Suddenly a voice near us roared, 'Get away from that car! That's stolen property!' A burly policeman was glowering at us.

I protested, 'It's my car, I'll show you my ownership papers.'

He wasn't interested. He escorted us to a room upstairs on the second floor where two plain-clothes policemen were seated, tough-looking men with hard faces. One squinted at me through his glasses as I placed my papers in front of him. He threw them back at me.

'Don't waste my time. Tell me about the contraband spirits you're carrying.'

I couldn't help laughing. 'We're carrying cooling water for my leaky radiator, that's all.' He got up and stuck our water container under my nose.

'Is this methylated spirits or not!'

'Put your finger in and taste it,' I suggested.

'Don't get smart with me, it's spirits alright. Where did you get it from?'

'The creek—it's creek water.' I persisted.

His red angry face was close and I expected to feel the force of one of his great fists and I was relieved when he stepped back.

'We'll have this substance analysed and you'll be locked up until we get the results,' he snarled.

We were put in a cell and there we waited for two hours before being released. We hadn't eaten since the previous day and treated ourselves to a hot meal. As we ate, Otto said he knew a major dealer in Berlin and wanted us to call on him. I had a feeling that he was up to no good and when we returned to the car, he pulled out a pistol.

He said to me, 'This man's got plenty of money lying around, it's easy to get hold of, we can fill our pockets. I'll stand over him and you can grab his cash.'

Otto was a tall, handsome man but I didn't like his eyes—they were light blue, like glass, you could look through them and know nothing of the man. I knew Otto well, we were both deserters but his was a different story. After one or two days away from his company, Otto's grandmother betrayed him to the military police. He was arrested and put in a concentration camp. He knew how to survive in the worst circumstances and came out of there after two years looking fit and well nourished.

A story circulated in Nienburg that he knew every boarding house in the town and went from one bedroom to the next bestowing his favours. A couple of times he finished up at the VD clinic but not before infecting his wife.

Finally Otto's philandering got too much for her and one day she followed him to the rail station at Nienburg where he was meeting his latest girlfriend. What her intentions were I don't know, but she pulled out a pistol from her handbag and fired a shot. The police arrested and gaoled her for discharging a pistol in a public place. Otto was gaoled for owning the pistol.

My connections with Otto were purely business but business without any rough stuff. I wasn't interested in using guns to threaten people or stealing from somebody. Selling items on the black market wasn't the same as stealing somebody's livelihood.

'I'm not interested in using stand-over tactics,' I told him. 'If I can't trade without that, I don't trade at all.'

Without a word, he put the pistol back in his pocket and I headed the truck home. That was the last time I had need of Otto's services.

At this time, because of extreme food shortages in East Germany, the Russians began ordering the Nienburg Council to round up all people born elsewhere and expel them. Because of the enormous number of displaced persons in Germany after the war, all nationalities, Poles, French, Yugoslavs were sent back to their homelands. My partner Hans was born close to Nienburg but, he had a Swiss father and Swiss identity papers. Although he told the authorities he had no connections in Switzerland (his Swiss father had died 20 years before), they said he must go back there. He had a wife and three children, all born in Nienburg but this carried no weight with the Russian authorities. There were no loopholes for Hans and I reluctantly farewelled him as he departed for Switzerland.

Unfortunately I have discovered that authority bears the same trademarks, no matter what nation wields it. Nazi authority gave Germans the right to move into Poland and take over land there. One such who benefited from the Nazi 'generosity' to German nationals was a contact man I met called Anton. He was a tall, fat, middle-class man who had lived in Schlesien in Poland for years and built up a business. After being dispossessed by the Russians, he began again, starting from scratch back in Germany.

Anton had all the connections he needed in Berlin, plenty of money from black market trading but he did not possess a truck. At this time, money was worth nothing, inflation was rampant, a truck worth 5,000 marks was priced at 25,000. Anton had a good nose; he could smell where the money was and he wanted me to work for him and carry black market goods. He sent Hans the money for his share of the truck but here his 'nose' let him down. I had not bothered to insure the vehicle and two months later, a driver I employed came to grief. Travelling on a road between Halle and Bernburg the truck skidded on black ice and crashed into a house, damaged beyond repair.

Anton was coldly furious with me. 'You're bankrupt material!' he snarled at me.

Maybe he was right, I had run out of money and had no transport. All I could think of was to contact Hans in Switzerland in the hope of getting some coffee from him to sell. I left home and got to the border between East and West Germany at a place called Konstanz. When I climbed over a three-strand wire fence, I was standing on Swiss soil. My goal was Waggis, 80 kilometres (50 miles) away where Hans lived. I was full of confidence after two years underground experience dodging the military police. On reaching the Waggis rail station, I had trouble reading the map so I asked an official which train to take.

Suddenly I was aware of somebody standing beside me. Of course it was a policeman.

He looked at me smugly, taking an official police badge from his coat pocket.

'What is your business in Waggis?'

'I am here to visit an old friend.'

'I know you're from Germany—you're under arrest.'

'What have I done wrong?'

'Every German needs a passport and a visa, show me yours and you're free to go. If you haven't ...' He clapped a heavy hand on my shoulder.

I am sure I entered the nicest gaol in existence—Swiss cheese for breakfast, a beautiful lunch and with every meal, a lovely strong aromatic cup of coffee such as you could get nowhere else. I was there a week when Hans came to see me, his eyes full of surprise and concern. I was delighted to see him. He was working as a labourer in a tourist town in the mountains and looked well.

'I never expected to see you in a Swiss gaol,' said Hans.

I laughed. 'Strange to say, I found it easier to fool the Nazi police, than the Swiss,' I replied, nodding towards a warder some distance away.

Hans was allowed only 10 minutes to talk to me and I explained quickly that I was broke, my truck smashed and could he help me with supplies of coffee. My old partner looked sorrowful and thrust his hand through the bars.

'This is not a nice place for us to meet again,' he said, grasping my hand strongly. 'I wish you all the best, Comrade!'

He left me, turning and waving his hand and I watched his familiar figure until he was out of sight. The Swiss police handed me over to the French border police in Germany. The border police searched me and found money I had hidden in my coat lining.

'It is a crime to smuggle money over the border,' they said. 'You have to pay 200 marks for this crime.'

As I didn't have it, I spent three months in a gaol at Lahr-Dinglingen. What a contrast from the last one, the food was pitiful, near starvation rations. For breakfast we had dry rye bread and burnt barley coffee; for lunch, thin lentil soup and at night, rye bread. I went down from 70 kilos (11 stone) to 53 kilos (8 stone). There were a hundred of us housed in a big shed, sleeping on double bunks. The French guards treated us with contempt, to them we were all ex-Nazis despite the fact that most of the inmates were in for border jumping, only a few were political prisoners.

Politics was not a subject we talked of often, but prison broke down barriers and we knew who among us were ex-Nazis. There was only one subject we talked about continuously. Food! How to make dumplings, how to cook fondue, what great meals we prepared for festivals. Sex was never mentioned!

MOVING TO WEST GERMANY

After the severity of my prison sentence, I felt reluctant to go back and live in East Germany under Russian military rule, I wanted to live permanently in the West. I wrote to Brunhilde and told her to sell up our furniture (we had some nice pieces) and my car. By doing that she managed to scrape together 200 dollars, which saved me spending another two months in gaol. A week before my release, Brunhilde got accommodation close at hand and brought me a handsome parcel of sausages, good loaves of bread, cheese and other choice items. My mates immediately were at my elbows and I had no choice but to share my food with them.

When I was released we took a train back to Essen in the Ruhr Valley and stayed with Brunhilde's brother Bernard. He had room for us in a house he bought from Krupp-Konzern housing estate. The owner, Baron von Krupp was sentenced to 15 years imprisonment for his part in building up Hitler's war machine. It made me cynical when

I learned he was released by the Allied Control Authority and served only a few months of this sentence. Not only that, he was given back all his properties, his factories and his cash assets and soon set up in business again. His regular money-earner, weapons production, was denied him and he switched to making household metal goods. When Bernard's house was returned to Krupp, he was refunded the sum of money he paid for it and thereafter lived in the house as Krupp's tenant.

By now, I was broke. I refused to live off my father-in-law's money that he earned the hard way in a coalmine. He still had a young brood to feed, so very soon I was back into black market dealing in foodstuffs. Food had been short during the war, external trade was disrupted and food items were not imported from other countries. The post-war situation was not much better, there was plenty of scope for black market trading

I rationalised, why not provide people with items impossible for them to get and make a modest profit for myself at the same time? I bought ration tea from the coalminers, who received 'care' packages of extra food from the American Quakers' organisation every three months to sustain their inadequate diet.

Word got around in Essen that trade goods were available in Oldenburg in the north-west. Oldenburg was the only place in Germany where the northerners drank tea, very strong with sugar and milk and it was there I went with a backpack full of precious tea to trade. I had an uncomfortable trip to Oldenburg by train, travelling with other people intent on doing a bit of small-time trading to supplement their unvaried diet.

Post-war transport was by no means back to normal and we stood squashed together for all of the journey. Some reckless souls perched on the buffers between carriages.

I got talking to an ex-Navy officer on the train, anything to pass the time in those uncomfortable cramped conditions. He told me I could find accommodation with an old lady who owned a large double-storey house in Oldenburg. This proved to be true. The old lady after reassuring herself I was respectable, gave me a room upstairs.

Next morning, I was up at dawn walking and hitching rides to some little villages 20 kilometres (12 miles) away. There I was able to obtain pork and butter from the farmers in exchange for tea. Sometimes I exchanged tea for potatoes and then I hoisted a hundredweight bag of potatoes onto the train for the return trip. It became a good business and I made the same trip every three months, selling the food to people in the Ruhr Valley.

ESCAPE FROM AN EAST GERMAN PRISON

On one trip I met Greta, a smartly dressed, well-educated, serious young woman in her late 20s who also had accommodation in the old lady's house. She told me she was from the south of East Germany and was trading stockings for butter and ham. She was friendly and promised to introduce me to contacts in the textile industry in Karl Marx Town in Saxony. Next day we travelled there by train and trade was indeed good, I was able to exchange butter and meat for 10 metres of the best suiting material. We stayed overnight in a hotel, my interest in Greta was purely business so after a few drinks we retired to our separate rooms.

A heavy knock sounded on my door just as I was about to get into bed. Two policemen stood outside and one of them, a sergeant demanded to see my identification card. I showed him my brother-in-law's I.D. card, my own I.D. card would have identified me as a citizen of East Germany. Living in the West was a crime in the eyes of the East German authorities and carried a gaol sentence.

'You live in West Germany! What are you doing here?'

'I'm travelling around, having a holiday with my girlfriend.'

The policeman looked grim. 'You could be a spy, you didn't come through the official checkpoint, you came over here without the proper authority!'

He was getting red-faced and shouted. 'We have ORDER in our country not like the decadent West! I'm arresting you as an illegal person!' He marched me out and I stayed overnight in a small prison cell behind the police station. The next morning I was taken under guard back to Karl Marx Town then to an old DKW car factory that had been converted into a prison camp.

I was put in an upstairs part of the old factory where 30 or 40 other prisoners were held. One large section served as a community room and another as a dormitory for all of us. During daytime hours, we were permitted to walk about in the yard and at night we were locked in the dormitory. We wore prison uniforms with a wide red triangle on the back of the jacket and heavy clumsily made wooden shoes. All of the other prisoners had been arrested on petty misdemeanours. As time wore on I felt very restless, there was no sign of a proper charge being laid against me and no fixed time for a court appearance. I couldn't take the risk of writing to Brunhilde or anyone using my false name. The food was poor and I felt very homesick. After six weeks, I'd had enough.

One morning I saw maintenance workmen had left a couple of planks extending from our building to the empty building on the other side. I immediately saw it was an escape route for me and with growing excitement I made plans. I found a piece of wire in the exercise yard, which I bent into a lock pick. When I tried it on one of the locked windows it worked. I was elated at the thought of escape and I told my particular mate, a tall skinny East German what I intended doing and he decided to come with me.

That night I went to bed fully clothed and barely slept, going through my plan to be sure it would work. As soon as the guards shouted their 'get up' order at 6 a.m. I was first out of bed, rousing my mate. 'Are you ready?'

'I changed my mind,' he said. I understood his situation. Unlike me he was an East German citizen and the police would easily pick him up. I went straight into the community room and discovered the workers had locked my escape window. I hastily unpicked the lock, acutely aware of passing time. Other prisoners came around me and stood with their mouths open.

'What are you doing?' one of them said.

'Just guess.' I pushed the window up and leapt onto the planks. I found they were good and solid and walked over them quickly and easily without looking down to the ground four metres below. When I found the window in the next building was locked I swung my arm and shattered the window glass with my elbow. The guard at the gate was pacing around without seeing me but the crash alerted him. He looked up shading his eyes in the early morning sun and began walking towards the building to investigate.

With as much haste as I could manage in my clumsy wooden shoes, I got to the outside stairs of the empty building, thumped down them and ran the length of the long yard to a gate at the bottom end. I spurred myself on through the gate, running down a long grassy hill. A flowing creek at the bottom didn't stop me—I splashed right in. The water flowed above my knees and suddenly I couldn't stand up, a numbing weakness came over me and I fell face down in the water. The icy water revived me and I staggered up and floundered onto the bank. I couldn't run anymore, I was exhausted and lay panting on the grass. Thoughts that the police would catch me, that I'd be dumped back in prison didn't move or worry me.

I recovered a little, got up and hurried on. Ahead of me lay a long line of private gardens, similar to Mother's, on the outskirts of the town. I climbed over the fence nearest me, tearing my trousers in nervous haste. I saw a garden house and made towards it, planning to disguise my appearance and rest safely for a few minutes, confident it was too early for anyone to be about. I hooked the tear in my trousers together with the bent lock pick, took off my jacket with the prisoners' red triangle, turned it inside out and tied it round my waist. During these adjustments, I failed to see an elderly man enter the garden gate.

'Aha, you're the thief,' he cried. 'Now I know who's been thieving my strawberries!' His cheeks flushed with triumph.

I laughed derisively. 'I don't want your bloody strawberries!' I guess I looked pretty desperate, gaunt of face with sodden clothes and a wild glint in my eyes. 'Tell me which way to get out of here without touching the highway!'

Whether he was frightened or whether he wanted to help I can't say, maybe I wasn't the first escaped prisoner to come his way, but he gave me the information I needed. 'Go through the forest for six kilometres and you'll come to the highway to Leipzig.' Off I went, thumping along the forest track in my heavy shoes, not having a thought or an eye for the beauty of the fresh dewy forest as I covered the distance.

On the highway I stopped the first vehicle travelling towards me, a truck with an obliging driver who set me down in Leipzig. I hailed another truck that took me as far as Halle where I stayed overnight, sleeping under a bush not far from the road. I felt satisfied with my progress—from there it was only 60 kilometres (37 miles) to the border. I picked up a lift in the morning and by then I was ravenous, I hadn't eaten for 24 hours. The truckie was a nice fellow and on reaching the border, he shared his lunch with me. I couldn't risk being seen crossing the East-West border during daylight hours, so I lay down on the grassy slopes with the sun shining on my face, content to wait until nightfall. It was a beautiful day and I was completely happy except for the gnawing hunger in my belly. Something prompted me to get up and go a little further to discover a wonderful sight, a cherry tree laden with beautiful fruit. I ran towards it and began picking and eating, shoving the fruit into my mouth. I ate and ate until my belly was full.

As it grew dark the moon rose and by its light I saw I had to head north-west. I walked all night, my heavy wooden shoes impeding my progress and blistering my feet so I took them off and walked in my socks. I covered 10 kilometres (6 miles) over a succession of big hills without resting and was heartened when the first faint glimmerings of dawn appeared. As the light strengthened, I saw a little town below me and soon knew it was a West German town. My innate sense of direction had not failed me—I had come safely over the border.

I made straight for the rail station, I had not a penny in my pocket and explained to the ticket official that I wanted to go home to Essen, but had no money for the fare. He took my address and advised me to pay at the rail station nearest to my home. I travelled all day in the train, then walked 3 kilometres. I felt spent but the thought of Brunhilde spurred me on. When I arrived home it was dark and she was already in bed. She bounced up, her eyes wide with astonishment.

'So you're back!' she cried, her voice trembling with emotion. 'Got sick of that woman you went off with, did you?' Her stormy eyes accused me as tears streamed down her cheeks. 'Go back to her! I don't want you!'

I was astonished at her passionate outcry, I had been anticipating a warm fond greeting and a happy reconciliation after such a long absence. 'Brunhilde, darling, listen to me, I just got out of prison, I escaped. Look at me!' I went close to her but she shrank back. 'I haven't been with any woman,' I held my arms out. 'See, I've lost all this weight, I was a prisoner for six weeks.' She gazed at me searchingly without speaking, trying to control her turbulent emotions.

She sobbed, 'That old woman you stayed with in Oldenburg, she told me you left with another woman, a young woman from East Germany.'

'So I did, she took me to some factories and I bought a lot of good stuff, then before I could come back with it I was arrested.' I moved closer to her. '*Herzchen* (sweetheart), I wanted to write and tell you but I was using a false name.' I put my arms around her and she sobbed out the pain and humiliation she had endured during the long lonely days. 'I knew you'd be wondering what had become of me, every day I was missing you, hoping I could come home to you.' I wiped the tears from her flushed cheeks. 'Did you really think I'd desert you?'

'Yes I did! That old lady couldn't tell me quick enough how Mr Trappman, went off with that other woman and didn't come back.' Brunhilde pouted her dislike. 'And she enjoyed telling me.' I laughed and clasped her warm body closer. I knew she believed me. Forget about food and wine, forget about adventures, there's nothing like the pleasure of one's own wife, six weeks I'd been without her and it felt like an eternity. I ripped my prison clothes off and leapt into bed with Brunhilde's soft arms around me.

Soon after I arrived home, the West German government brought in new currency to bring down the soaring inflation and everyone was given 40 marks. Brunhilde and I felt suddenly rich and hopped on a train to Essen for a good day out. We saw an advertisement in a restaurant window, 'Snails in Aspic'. They were costly but as this was something special we immediately went in and ordered a plate each. They were tough like rubber and completely tasteless, in other words totally inedible. We paid for them and left for home where we filled our empty stomachs with a good meal of our usual hot potato pancakes.

SELLING, SELLING, BUT NEVER GETTING RICH

After my wasted time in prison, I badly needed some ready cash to get us out of the 'red'. I began making schnapps with the bare minimum of ingredients, 50 kilograms (8 stone) of sugar from our local grocer and sufficient yeast from the local baker. All I had in the way of brewing vessels was a 200 litre-container (53 gallons) smelling strongly of herrings. No matter how much I washed and scrubbed, the fishy smell hung on. Surprisingly, the product turned out first class, with a 32 per cent alcohol content. I sold some to the local publican and the rest to the miners in their 'colony' of company houses.

Six weeks after escaping from prison, the East German police traced me to my abode in the West. Heinz, Brunhilde's young brother arrived in great haste on his bicycle one morning, breathless and bearing important news. 'A policeman has been at Franz's house looking for you,' he puffed. 'Franz told him where you are and he'll be here any minute.'

'Where is he now?'

Heinz pointed down the street to a square-shouldered bulky figure approaching. I knew there was nothing to gain by trying to dodge him, so I walked toward him saying, 'I'm Bruno Trappmann.' His eyes held the characteristic penetrating stare of every policeman I have ever encountered.

'You've led us quite a dance,' the policeman confessed. He didn't produce handcuffs and I could sense his manner was rather relaxed.

'Come into my house, we can talk there.' He nodded his square head and followed me in. We settled down comfortably over a cup of coffee, our visitor acting very politely to Brunhilde and making a real effort to coax little Marlies out from behind her mother's skirts.

'Do you know why I'm here?' he began.

'I crossed over the border without the proper papers,' I ventured. He nodded and wanted to know all the details, which he laboriously wrote down. On completion, he pushed it across the table and ordered me to sign. Lighting a cigarette, he squinted at me through the smoke, the hardness in his gaze dissolving in a spark of humour.

'I'll tell you something young man. In your shoes I would have done the same thing. These are uncertain days and we have to get through the best we can.' We showed our gratitude with freshly brewed coffee and cakes. As he sat enjoying the snacks, he suddenly straightened and sniffed the air. 'Ah … I can smell something and I think I know what it is.' I had forgotten about my 200 litres of schnapps and its characteristic odour strongly assailed our nostrils.

'It's the summer temperature,' I said quickly, 'There's always a fermenting odour floating around in summer time.'

His mouth twisted into a grin. 'You can't fool me, it smells like you're making schnapps.' He got up and leisurely stretched his thick body. 'Don't worry, I'm not here for that.' He held out his big fleshy hand. 'Good luck but be careful, don't take any more risks, the law doesn't bend for adventurers like you.' With a sense of relief I closed the door behind him and went to check on my schnapps. I had to get rid of it, I hadn't been charged but they could come and confiscate it at any time. I spread the word around and customers queued up for supplies and once more we were in the money.

I looked around for a suitably private place to make fresh supplies. A man known in the town by the name of 'Adolph' (he groomed a small moustache of black whiskers) owned a good house with a high fence and a big roomy shed. When I sounded him out, he was enthusiastic, 'No one will interfere with you, but don't go near my dog, he'll tear your leg off!' Certainly the dog frothed and snarled and barked in a frenzy when I came in the gate but it was all a bluff. As soon as he was off the chain, he became as docile as a mouse, a bit like his owner. Adolph and I began making schnapps on a larger scale.

For a steady income, I needed to have a variety of products ready to sell at the numerous carnivals held in each town. To make roll mops (a popular product) I took a herring fillet, placed a gherkin and an onion in the centre, rolled it up and used a tooth pick to hold the lot together. Adolph came in with me and we sold them over a 200 kilometre (124 miles) radius. I have been a lucky fellow all my life but I did have my share of problems to solve. At this time, I bought a barrel of herrings from a lady (shaped like a barrel) at the wholesale market. When I got it home, I discovered the oil was rancid. I took it back.

'They're no good,' I told the fish lady.

'They were good when I sold them to you, why didn't you tell me then?'

'How could I? The barrel was sealed.'

'Too bad, a deal's a deal! I'm not taking them back!' So there I was with 200 kilograms (31½ stone) of good herrings in rancid oil. I decided to drain off the oil and put the fish in a solution of vinegar and water laced with pepper and mustard seeds. After leaving them for a week, they were completely toothsome and saleable. My time as a pastry cook taught me how to make the best of my mistakes and leftovers.

Marlies, on her first day of school.

My next venture was in smoked fish. My mother-in-law had been on a trip to Bremerhaven, the fishing port and came back with a bagful of delicious smoked fish. We couldn't eat enough of them. I could 'smell' a good business in these fish and decided to buy a few hundred kilograms each week. Early next day I took Brunhilde and little Marlies with me to the fishing port. We rented a place with one room and a cooking alcove.

When we settled in, I found the man I wanted, a wharf labourer who handled loads of fish coming off the boats. Every day I bought quantities from him and put them on the train back to Essen where Bernard, my brother-in-law, sold them on the open market. One of the wharfies had facilities to smoke the fish and invited me to use his large smoke oven.

'Do enough for both of us!' It was a good tasty product and customers were delighted to add this appetising dish to their unvaried diet. For three months I traded smoked fish, then the demand began to taper off as more food appeared in the shops with a larger variety to choose from.

One particular incident happened concerning my sister Hilde during this time. In 1948 she was working for the East German Council under Russian supervision and I was selling herrings on the black market in Magdeburg. While in the East, I stayed at my sister Lore's place. One day on returning to Nienburg, I was surprised to see Mother at the Calbe station where I changed trains.

'What are you doing here, Mother? Why are you dressed in black?' She had not worn black since Father died and I could tell she was very upset.

'Hilde may be your sister, but she is no longer a daughter of mine,' she told me in a low terse voice. 'I've cast her out. I am wearing black because I have lost a daughter! She has notified the police of your activities and they came and arrested Brunhilde. Now the police are out looking for you this very moment!' I learned later that the police went to Lore's place with a search warrant. They searched through her house, making a thorough job of it, going into each bedroom and feeling the beds to see if any of them were warm.

'You can't go back to Nienburg,' Mother said. 'They will arrest you, they're holding Brunhilde so they can catch you.' The police let Brunhilde go the next day and she and Mother waited another day, then caught the train to Magdeburg. We all celebrated that night and said some hard words about Hilly but I never was able to hold a grudge against my sister and Mother wasn't wearing black for long. Years later, when I built up a lucrative business in scrap iron in the Black Forest, time and distance separated me from Mother. Our happy family evening together in Magdeburg was sadly the last time I saw her. When I left Germany, thousands of kilometres of oceans separated us until her death in 1956.

In June 1948, West Berlin was blockaded by the Russians who wanted to put a stop to any produce coming in from West Germany. It was a soaring sellers' market and I went to the wholesale market in Brunswick and looked around for something cheap to buy. I saw boxes of lemons and knew they were fetching a hundred times their price in Berlin due to the Russian blockade but I also knew that prices could fall overnight. Brunhilde and I wasted no time and set off with a quantity of fruit. When I needed an extra pair of hands, Brunhilde was my companion and helper.

I had the best part of a hundredweight of lemons on my back in a rucksack and Brunhilde carried a smaller pack. We crossed the border and caught a train to the western heart of Berlin, 250 kilometres (155 miles) away. I found my way around the city easily and selected a dealer I knew. He was not the only one, traders were everywhere on the lookout for goods. The blockade made it possible to sell any item of food, but this situation did not last. The West Germany economy was improving rapidly due to backing from the U.S. dollar.

After we collected our 'lemon' money, Brunhilde looked around with appreciative eyes at the attractive displays in the brightly lit shops. 'Let's have a promenade,' she said. I knew that meant a shopping spree. I wanted to save the money and put it back into business, but Brunhilde had an eye for lovely clothes and soon she emerged from dress shops, carrying parcels and wearing a new frock.

One day, when I was alone on the 'lemon run', a well-dressed middle-aged lady sat across from me in the railway carriage travelling to Berlin. She introduced herself and admitted she was in the trading business.

Her husband, a top Nazi had worked for Himmler's deputy in the SS and had been murdered by a Yugoslav with a score to settle after Germany had surrendered. Whatever I thought to the contrary, in Frau Sattler's eyes, her husband was a good man. She admitted that her income came from black market trading and that she was looking for a trading partner.

I expressed interest and she invited Brunhilde and I to stay at her place in Berlin near the Tempelhof airport—it was the air bridge between West Germany and West Berlin. Every four minutes a plane roared over the roof, preparing to land, and for the first few nights, it was impossible for us to sleep.

Frau Sattler and I decided to put in equal money and work together trading on the black. I told her I would buy knackers (sausages filled with a fresh smoked and spiced meat) and deliver them to Berlin via Schenker and Company, one of the biggest transport firms in Germany. Everything went well, we were making money and selling gigantic quantities.

One day the truck packed with sausages overturned near Magdeburg, the goods spilling out onto the road. Suddenly people came rushing forward from everywhere, grabbing handfuls of sausages. East German people hadn't seen them for years and by the time Brunhilde and I arrived on the scene, there was not a sausage in sight. All my money was invested in the load. I sought out Frau Sattler, thinking there was a chance we could get insurance money to cover the loss.

'No Bruno,' she said, 'It was a "private goods" consignment and as such, not covered.' I was half inclined to think she was holding back on me, the insurance contract was in her name. That was the end of our partnership. I worked for her for a few more weeks having no immediate prospects.

When I came back from West Berlin one day, she called me in and I knew something had upset her. She didn't offer me a chair and confronted me with flashing eyes.

'Your wife has been spreading rumours about me.'

'I don't believe Brunhilde would do that.'

'Oh yes, she's been telling people we are having a love affair.'

I looked at her in surprise and said emphatically, 'But that's impossible!' She flushed and gave her head a haughty toss.

'Is it impossible, is it REALLY impossible?'

I knew she was offended and said hurriedly, 'It's completely impossible for Brunhilde to make up stories like that.' My attempt to repair her sense of injury was useless. Her pride was badly wounded. She continued trading but without me, the employee who proved not susceptible to her charms!

When the Berlin blockade ended, black market trading nosedived; trucks began getting through from West Germany to supply West Berlin with all kinds of food selling at reasonable prices. It was time to look for another way of making money.

In the meantime, Brunhilde and I toured around setting up stalls at carnivals and selling anything I could get hold of. A man at a stall next to us had a large cheese shaped like a mighty circular wheel and weighing about one and a half hundredweight. I was surprised when he said to me, 'Here! Make me an offer, I'm sick of selling cheese!'

I bought it and we sold cheese for several months, living in an upstairs flat at the back of Burda's printshop in Offenburg. One day, after long hours of trading, I felt weary and disinclined to lug the heavy cheese up the stairs. Instead, I covered it and left it on a bench in the back yard. Next morning it was gone. I called in the detectives— the cheese was worth a lot of money. They investigated and said two workers from Burda's had put my cheese in a safe place in the cellar and it had been stolen from there. I knew I'd done a stupid thing but I applied to the Court to get compensation without success. The magistrate told me what I already knew—I had made a gift of the cheese to thieves.

The time had come to move from my brother-in-law's house in Essen. I wanted more freedom to go from place to place, buying cheap goods. My friend Mick Heinze said he knew of a vast factory that made mint-flavoured sweets. We saw the manager, a conservatively dressed man who spoke in a quiet voice. He told us coldly that he had proper connections and outlets and wasn't interested in supplying us. I think he suspected we would sell his sweets on the black market and give him a bad reputation.

When we walked away from his factory, we passed a well set-up butcher shop, which suddenly reminded me of Uncle Karl. This uncle arranged for a country butcher to send him a parcel of the best quality sausages every month. Each butcher in every country town made sausages and we entered this one's shop and made a deal. His best sausages were 'knackers' and people in Berlin were mad about them, heating them up and eating them like frankfurts. After a while our butcher began selling us poor-grade goods and so that was that.

I obtained a flat at the edge of the Black Forest and wrote to Brunhilde to join me. She arrived a week later with a Leica camera she had bought with the last of our money. Good cameras were extremely hard to get and I knew I could sell it easily. My contacts steered me towards a wealthy man, Herr Wolfe, who unbeknownst to me, was a crook. He took the camera eagerly.

'I'll give you the money in three weeks,' he told me, and then disappeared.

I went to the Court and laid charges against him. The bailiffs discovered he had stripped his house of everything of value. An old Persian carpet full of gaping holes was all I was given. Herr Wolfe lived up to his name!

We had no money, I was fed up with trading and getting nowhere, so I took a job as a store man at Emil Fischer, the biggest textile shop in Offenburg, and worked for them all winter. I was poorly paid, 50 marks a week and to supplement my wage, I gave blood to the hospital blood bank once a month. It was worth 50 marks, the amount I worked for the whole week. Occasionally when we were broke, I turned up at the hospital early. The medical staff would look at me sternly and say, 'You shouldn't be here so soon.'

'But I am here,' I would reply. I needed the money and they needed the blood, so they took it from me.

After the spell at Emil Fischer's, I got itchy feet, so off we went with a hundredweight bag of nutmegs to try our luck. We travelled around in a 200-kilometre (124-mile) circle, selling at open markets. I sold three nutmegs for one mark and gave away a balloon with each purchase. Little Marlies wanted to help and called out in her childish voice, 'Three nutmegs and a balloon extra.' As you can imagine we didn't make a fortune from that venture.

BANKRUPT

Brunhilde was close to having our second child so we got a larger flat where our son Bernard was born. With the family growing, I needed to make more money and I heard there was plenty of cash to be made from scrap iron. Factories in the south of the Black Forest had supplies of it and Junghans, the biggest watch factory, was one of them. Another, the Werle factory in Furtwangen, was making cuckoo clocks and I bought a lot of MS 56, a brass mixture of special quality used in the manufacture of clocks. I got top money for it, six to seven dollars a kilogram and sold it to a smelter living in the Black Forest. There were other metal factories making bolts and screws so there was plenty of scrap metal to be had for anyone with a vehicle.

While I was wandering around checking out the best factories to deal with, I met a group of gypsies. I liked gypsies, they had lots of vitality, seeming to spark it off each other. One of them, Henry Beerhandle, was of particular interest to me, as he had an old utility van. We loaded up his vehicle with scrap from the nearest factory and delivered it to a wholesale yard. There was no shortage of metal, the money was good and most of the factory owners were very happy to deal with me. It was cash-in-hand which meant no tax for them. The gypsies knew the whereabouts of a lot of factories but they were barred from coming through the gates. I was their front man and the profits we made we shared among us.

I was quite satisfied with the way things were going, the gypsies worked in well with me but they were easily offended. Once Brunhilde innocently referred to them as 'gypsies' and they didn't speak to her for a week. A couple hundred of them lived permanently on the outskirts of Offenburg in poor housing. Some went around farms searching for old farm implements, which was another source of scrap metal. One day Henry's brother-in-law asked me for 200 dollars. 'I've got plenty of iron for you,' he said. I gave him the money and waited and waited and finally he turned up empty-handed.

'Where's my scrap iron?' I asked. He shrugged his shoulders and didn't answer me.

Henry said, 'Bruno, why did you give him money? I could have told you, you'll never get it back.'

During this time we were living in Furtwangen hotel in the middle of winter and our car became buried deep under the snow. We were snowed in for a fortnight. There was nothing to do but mingle with other people and drink spicy hot *glühwein* (mulled wine) and look out the window at the falling snow. On Saturdays and Sundays there was dancing and lots of convivial company. As a ploy to attract tourists, everything at the hotel was reduced to a dollar, all meals and overnight accommodation.

When we were once more free to move around I was tipped off to go to Oberndorf. The once highly profitable Mauser factory, where they made Mauser rifles, lay in ruins. It had been totally destroyed by Allied bombing and there were tonnes and tonnes of cables lying around, a rich source of copper wire and aluminium.

Taking it easy at home.

My scrap iron business ran for three years. I bought two trucks to carry full loads from the factories to the wholesaler. Financially I was going very well, almost all the factories in the Black Forest were selling their scrap to me. Henry Beerhandle and his gypsy friends came over from time to time from Offenburg with additional supplies.

One day Alfonse Fischer, one of my workers, asked me to lend him my five-tonne truck. He had uncovered a further great heap of discarded cables rusting away at the Mauser factory. Alfonse said, 'If we don't grab it, somebody else will.'

I gave him the truck and he and his mate left, the plan being to bring it back full next morning. In the middle of the night I was wakened out of a deep sleep by somebody bashing at the door. I had the feeling all was not well and sure enough, two police stood at the front door.

'Mr Trappmann, get dressed and come with us to the police station,' one said.

'What is this about?'

'You know I think.'

'I don't.'

'Where is your truck?'

'I gave it to one of my workers.'

'All right, come with us, you have to make a statement. It's a very strange thing—you gave your truck away and you don't know anything.' I explained that I give my truck to people to buy material, but not to steal it. 'That's the way I handle my business.'

The police weren't satisfied but they had no evidence against me so had to let me go. Alphonse and his mate were already behind bars having been caught in the act. The Court case came on and my two workers were given a sentence of two months gaol, but fortunately this was suspended by the magistrate and they were placed on a good behaviour bond.

While we were staying at Oberndorf, we made many friends. One was Fritz, a tall, slim, young man with a young family. He was head of the local fire brigade and an expert with explosives. After the war he earned good money demolishing what was left of dangerous buildings—an aftermath of Allied bombing. Life was treating him well, he had a pleasant young wife and healthy children who were often at our place.

All that changed when one of the publicans offered him a lot of money to burn his hotel down. Fritz agreed to the stupid plan, bought quantities of petrol and one Sunday night set fire to the pub, burning it to the ground. He carelessly left some empty petrol tins on site. On Monday morning when he visited us for his usual cup of coffee, he was talking in a strange way. He sighed heavily and I saw tears in his eyes as he looked at our little children and remarked sadly, 'I've got a lovely young family just as you have.' Brunhilde and I couldn't understand his strange mood, we knew nothing of what he had done.

I said, 'Bring your children over today, they can all play here together.'

He turned his face away without answering. Later that day we heard that he had been arrested by the police for arson and faced a lengthy prison term. Immediately we understood his strange mood.

At this time, without warning, my financial world split apart. Germany joined the Mountain Union and the price of metal went dramatically down. The Mountain Union was a big organising body for capitalist plants handling raw iron. Prices plummeted from 135 marks to 55 marks per tonne. It broke me and everyone else in the business.

I was in a quandary—for me to sell material I had bought for 100 dollars a tonne for 55 dollars was impossible. While I was trying to work out a solution, an agent knocked at my door.

'Mr Trappmann, I saw quantities of your iron lying on the ramp at the rail station. So much scrap iron! What are you doing with it all?'

I looked sceptically at this busybody, knowing he would want the scrap at bargain basement prices. 'There's no way I'm selling the stuff to you at 55 dollars a tonne!'

'No, no, quite right, I wouldn't expect you to. I'm from Bauer's, you've heard of them, the leading scrap iron company. We'll pay you 100 dollars per tonne, we've got contracts and can pay you that price.' What he said did a lot to lift my spirits, if I could at least sell my stocks, I could then go into some other kind of business.

'O.K.' I said, 'I'll start loading tomorrow.' When he left I went straight to the rail station and ordered 10 railway lorries. I joined my gang of five men and worked the whole week, filling the lorries. Most of the loads were between 20 and 25 tonnes and I consigned them all to Bauer's in the Ruhr Valley. I spent the last of my money buying more scrap to fill even more lorries. When I was down to my last mark, I went to see Mr Rapp, my bank manager, to increase my overdraft. He sat back in his chair and gave me a penetrating look.

'I heard the bottom has fallen out of the scrap iron business, I am very doubtful if I can give you another loan.' I assured him I had a good contract and was getting close to the right price for my metal. 'Tell me the firm,' he said, 'I will check it out and if everything's alright, I will advance you money.'

When he rang me early next morning and told me to come to the bank straight away, I was certain it was to arrange a loan for me. He looked at me with a grim face from behind his big desk and I knew something was wrong.

'Mr Trappmann,' he began, 'I've got bad news for you, the first thing I have to tell you is that Bauer's are bankrupt. The next thing, we can't advance you any credit and the last is that your overdraft has to be paid back immediately.' He sat back and watched my reactions. My face burned, my heart was pounding with anger. I got up without a word to him and went out. What could I say or do? I had nothing in my pockets. There was only one move left and Brunhilde and I decided to have a showdown with Bauer's manager. We came straight into his large office, ignoring his secretary, who tried to intervene. He was the typical head man, towering and prosperous-looking, clean shaven, hair immaculately parted, shirt and suit of the best quality.

'Mr Bauer,' I said, 'You have large quantities of my scrap iron in your possession. I need advance money to buy more material for you.'

There was an unpleasant smile on his lips, he obviously knew what we were about and made no invitation for us to sit down. 'You'll have to wait, I'm sending you the money in a fortnight,' he said.

'It's not for me,' I persisted, keeping up the charade. 'It's to buy material for your business.'

He repeated, with a wave of his flabby white hand, 'I can't pay you today. You have to wait a fortnight.'

Brunhilde was boiling with emotion and couldn't remain silent any longer. She exploded, 'You owe us money, you've got all our metal! What you are doing is fraud, we're going straight from here to the police station.'

He rose immediately to his feet and pointed to the door. 'Leave my premises immediately or I'll ring the police and have you removed from them!' I tugged at Brunhilde's hand but she was loath to leave.

'It's fraud, nothing but fraud, the police should charge you for theft!' she yelled as he advanced around his desk to throw us out. We immediately went to the police station to charge Herr Bauer with double-dealing, but there was no justice to be had there. The police officer told me it was not a police matter, it had to be dealt with in the Civil Court.

'Better get yourself a good solicitor,' he advised me. Later, as I thought over the events of that disastrous day, my mind turned to the idea of migrating. It wasn't the first time I had thought about it and now with all my problems, it became a much more attractive proposition than waiting around for the result of a long and tedious court case that did not promise to deliver any positive outcome. I knew the bank manager would insist on the immediate repayment of the thousands I owed. Without money, I had no hope of starting another business, and all the capital I owned, all my material was in Herr Bauer's yard. That high-class crook never sent me a cent.

So that was it, there was no way out, the only thing was to get on a boat and leave my country. On the way home I met one of my workers and told him the whole story.

He said, 'Don't worry Bruno, we'll go to the pub tonight and see the publican, he knows all about migrating.'

'Alf, I haven't even beer money on me.'

'Don't worry, we'll play cards and I'm sure to win, that will pay for our beer.' I took him at his word and left Brunhilde home with the kids, wondering and worrying what was going to happen to us. I pumped the publican for all the information he had on migration.

'Go to the Australian Embassy in Hanau, Bavaria,' he advised me. 'By the way, the trip won't cost you a cent, Australia wants all the migrants it can get.'

Straight away we applied for passports and had our medical check up at the Embassy. Before me I could see the wide ocean and a big new continent where I could start life again without any record of black marketing or hopping national borders held against me. But I wasn't in the clear yet. One morning, two police picked me up in the shopping centre. 'What are you arresting me for?' I growled, extremely irritated at being detained yet again.

'I'm not arresting you, we have to bring you to the Taxation Office.' Another bit of petty officialdom, I thought, well, soon I'd be out. The Tax Commissioner was sitting in his swivel chair, looking important.

'Mr Trappmann,' he began, referring to papers in front of him. 'You have lived in Oberndorf for more than one year and you have ignored us.' He looked at me coolly. 'And now you are on the brink of leaving the country.' His lips twitched in a smile. 'But you will find you cannot, we have stopped your passports.' I began to see the inside; it looked as though, once again, my chosen path was blocked.

Circumstances had stripped me of everything I owned but I wasn't going to give up without a battle. I needed a new chance and moving to a new country far away could give it to me. I fixed my eyes intently upon this man who could give me a clear passage or deny it to me.

'Everything has two sides, I want to tell you my side.' He leaned back in his chair and I could tell he was prepared to listen. With my voice shaking with the indignation and emotion I felt, I told him what caused my financial collapse and the hopes I had of building a new future. My tense fingers yanked out of my pocket our health certificates with photos of Brunhilde and the children on them, laying them in front of him, hoping it would carry weight. He heard me out, without uttering a word.

'You and your wife have a lovely young family, Mr Trappmann,' he said, gazing at our photos. Suddenly he swung out of his swivel chair and turned his back to me. 'Look,' he said, 'I'm closing one eye and now I'm closing both eyes.' He turned round and thrust out a friendly hand, his face alight with a genial smile. 'Young man, I wish you the very best for your future in your new country, but I have this to say,' he added, holding up a warning finger. 'Whenever you come back, we will be the first ones to ask you for money.' I heaved a sigh of relief, thanked him and raced home to tell Brunhilde the good news.

SAYING GOODBYE

A fortnight later, we were on board the *Anna Salen*, a Swedish ship. We had packed up our light belongings and left the rest, my two trucks and my car, parked outside our lodgings. We just walked away, my financial loss was too much, a new life awaited us and I set my will against looking backwards. There were 1,200 of us migrants and a band on the wharf played our German farewell song, 'Bye bye my old country, one day I'll come home again.'

I stood on the deck for a long while and watched as the distance lengthened between my homeland and me. I joined Brunhilde on the lower deck, my heart beating to the tempo of the little town where I grew up. Sad thoughts filled my mind, when would I ever again see Mother and my sisters, with several vast oceans separating us?

We were more than three miles out when suddenly the engines cut out. There was something awesome in the unusual silence. We could hear the waves slapping up against the bows of the ship. Why this sudden stop to our journey, I wondered, but no explanation was given. Next morning however, it was the chief topic of conversation. One lady passenger, who had to know everything about everybody, had questioned the chief steward. She stopped me and said with a knowing smile, 'You must be so happy.'

Wondering at this remark, I replied, 'Of course I'm happy.'

'But you must be especially happy,' she insisted with a malicious glint in her eyes. I didn't understand her meaning, but it soon became clear. As we made our way to the dining hall to breakfast, the chief steward beckoned me to his office. He told me an order had come over the ship's radio from the German police to offload my family and me. The captain had argued his ship was outside the three-mile limit and therefore German law did not apply. I marvelled at my good luck and felt like kissing the ship's captain for helping me slip through German officialdom's net. I was free of them for the last time!

My pockets were empty but my heart was full of love and gratitude for my chance to make a new life for myself in a new country, free from the constraints I'd felt my whole life.

EPILOGUE

I am now 80 years of age, I have passed the millennium. I am living in the bosom of nature. Life is not yet over for me. I have plenty of things of interest around me, I am occupied from morning till night. I cook, I bake bread and cakes (I have become famous for my black forest cakes throughout the district) and I instruct Nancy, my second wife, on how to make our fruit wine. Our life here is ideal, we have water from gravity tanks, free electricity, clean air, bird song and the beauty of our trees all around us.

My life after leaving Germany wasn't easy. My family and I experienced culture shock moving to Australia. I also found it difficult, initially, to learn the language. Brunhilde and I were divorced and she passed away in 1973. While travelling to attend the second wedding of my daughter, Marlies, I met my second partner Nancy at a jazz show. I sensed that life with Nancy would be peaceful and harmonious, I loved her with all my heart and knew I had found the right comrade with whom to share the rest of my life. We found our own piece of paradise on a 300-acre block of land with a large, dilapidated house on it.

After the war, Hilde fell in love with Armonde, a French musician and spent the rest of her life with him, touring around Spain and Italy, enjoying the beauty and culture of other European countries. She kept her own flat, retaining her independence and being financially independent all the years she spent with Armonde. Despite all her fluctuations in political beliefs and romantic adventures, I was very fond of Hilde; when I migrated to Australia, I kept up an unbroken correspondence with her until she died at the age of eighty four.

In a reflective mood.

Hilde and Armonde.

I would like to end this account of my life by putting down the things that in retrospect I think are vitally important. I learned a lot as I travelled through life and I want to show people how pleasurable a more simple life can be without cutting trees and without relying on huge amounts of gas or coal or petrol.

My own experiences have taught me we have, to be peaceful to each other all over the world. Life is a gift, it has been given to us to live in peace with all the other creatures and we have to use it in the best way possible to fulfil ourselves and to be tolerant and generous to others we meet.

Looking ahead into the 21st century, I want a world of peace without weapons, so people of all races can live together, solving their differences without war.

I want people to be able to shape their futures without relying on selfish power-hungry leaders. Adolph Hitler showed the world what terrible depths the human race descended into. As a German, I am very conscious of my country's acceptance of the Nazi regime and the heinous crimes committed during its reign. I am proud I can say I opted out of Hitler's army and never ever in thought or deed supported his inhuman racist ideology.

Picking flowers in his 'paradise' with Nancy.

Bruno's progeny—sons John and Bruno Jnr, first and second left. Daughters-in-law Sandra and Dianne, son-in-law Gurd, grand-daughter Peggy, grand-son-in-law Will, and daughter Marlies. In front, Bruno Jnr and Sandra's three children, left, John and Dianne's two children, right. Bernard, Bruno's eldest son, is not pictured.

Acknowledgements

Thank you to Dr Keith Wilson, Marcia Bracken, Loma Thompson, Sue Tonkin, Stephanie Deutchbein, Shirley Russell, Fred Kaminski and members of the Astoria Club.

About the author

Nancy Inglis ... nurse; mother; environmental and social activist; historian, winemaker, poet; writer. On her property 'Koongoora' she has been a registered nurse and had a family before she met Bruno Trappmann in a jazz club in the 1970s. They established a farm together, making and selling cherry wine. She has a degree with honours in history and has previously published a poetry book.

First published in 2013 by
New Holland Publishers
London • Sydney • Cape Town • Auckland
www.newhollandpublishers.com • www.newholland.com.au

Garfield House 86–88 Edgware Road London W2 2EA United Kingdom
1/66 Gibbes Street Chatswood NSW 2067 Australia
Wembley Square First Floor Solan Road Gardens Cape Town 8001 South Africa
218 Lake Road Northcote Auckland New Zealand

A catalogue record of this book is available at the British Library and at the
National Library of Australia.

ISBN: 9781742574301

10 9 8 7 6 5 4 3 2 1

Managing director: Fiona Schultz
Publisher: Patsy Rowe
Project editor: Jodi De Vantier
Designer: Tracy Loughlin
Production director: Olga Dementiev
Printer: Toppan Leefung Printing Limited

Follow New Holland Publishers on
Facebook: www.facebook.com/NewHollandPublishers